T0178738

The Ace and Aro
Relationship Guide

by the same author

I Am Ace
Advice on Living Your Best Asexual Life
Cody Daigle-Orians
ISBN 978 1 83997 262 1
eISBN 978 1 83997 263 8

of related interest

Hopeless Aromantic
An Affirmative Guide to Aromanticism
Samantha Rendle
ISBN 978 1 83997 367 3
eISBN 978 1 83997 368 0

Ace and Aro Journeys
A Guide to Embracing Your Asexual or Aromantic Identity
The Ace and Aro Advocacy Project
ISBN 978 1 83997 638 4
eISBN 978 1 83997 639 1

Ace Voices
What it Means to Be Asexual, Aromantic, Demi or Grey-Ace
Eris Young
ISBN 978 1 78775 698 4
eISBN 978 1 78775 699 1

Sounds Fake But Okay
An Asexual and Aromantic Perspective on Love,
Relationships, Sex, and Pretty Much Anything Else
Sarah Costello and Kayla Kaszyca
ISBN 978 1 83997 001 6
eISBN 978 1 83997 002 3

The ACE and ARO Relationship Guide

MAKING IT WORK IN FRIENDSHIP, LOVE, AND SEX

CODY DAIGLE-ORIANS

Jessica Kingsley Publishers
London and Philadelphia

First published in Great Britain in 2025 by Jessica Kingsley Publishers
An imprint of John Murray Press

1

Copyright © Cody Daigle-Orians 2025

The right of Cody Daigle-Orians to be identified as the Author of the Work has been
asserted by them in accordance with the Copyright, Designs and Patents Act 1988.

Content Warning: This book mentions homophobia, transphobia, toxic relationships, and sex.

A CIP catalogue record for this title is available from the
British Library and the Library of Congress

ISBN 978 1 83997 734 3
eISBN 978 1 83997 735 0

Printed and bound in the United States by Integrated Books International

Jessica Kingsley Publishers' policy is to use papers that are natural, renewable and recyclable
products and made from wood grown in sustainable forests. The logging and manufacturing
processes are expected to conform to the environmental regulations of the country of origin.

Jessica Kingsley Publishers
Carmelite House
50 Victoria Embankment
London EC4Y 0DZ

www.jkp.com

John Murray Press
Part of Hodder & Stoughton Ltd
An Hachette Company

★ ★ ★

For David and Glinda, my mom and dad.
Thank you for always believing in me
and in all of my possibilities.

Contents

A User's Manual for The Ace and Aro Relationship Guide

Hi, friend. I'm glad you're here.

More than three years ago, I started Ace Dad Advice, a social media-based asexuality education project with two goals: to teach the basics of asexuality to those who are curious or confused, and to encourage people exploring asexuality to do so confidently while living their best ace lives. Over the years, the project has grown to include educational information about being aromantic and agender, as well.

It's been an incredible journey. In the online space, I've talked to thousands of folks across the globe in the asexual and aromantic communities about their lives, and they've shared their fears, their insecurities, their triumphs, and their joys. I've also had the pleasure of taking Ace Dad Advice into the world. I've spoken at universities about asexual and aromantic lives, and I've worked with companies and nonprofits to help their employees steward more ace- and aro-inclusive space.

And the coolest thing: Ace Dad Advice spawned a book! *I Am Ace: Advice on Living Your Best Asexual Life* is an Ace 101 guide filled with all the basics, some personal stories from my ace life, and a lot of advice and encouragement on how to be the best ace version of yourself.

The book has taken me to universities and independent bookstores across the United States, where I've gotten to meet amazing ace and aro readers and share joyful community space with them.

All that's been a lot of fun, but the real work of Ace Dad Advice is answering questions. Every day, I get messages from people everywhere looking for advice. While a large number of those questions deal with some of the identity basics—labels, attraction, coming out—the type of questions I get asked most are about relationships.

How do I tell someone I'm interested in that I'm ace or aro? Should I tell them upfront? Am I lying if I withhold the information for a while? How do I get them to respect my boundaries around intimacy? What if I don't want intimacy at all? Can I ask for a relationship if I don't want the kind they want? Is it selfish to pursue a relationship if I don't want romance? Will anyone ever want to be with me at all because I'm ace or aro?

These questions are not only the source of deep anxiety and frustration, but they limit the heights that ace and aro folks believe they can reach for in their lives. These questions make us believe that we should settle for less, and I firmly believe that we deserve *more*. Not only do we deserve the space to fully and authentically live our ace or aro identity within ourselves, but we deserve the space to joyfully share it with others in relationships.

So before we get to the relationship nitty-gritty, I want to provide a little user's manual for this book. If you're here, you're probably looking for some relationship wisdom, so I want to make sure you're in the right place and you find what you're looking for.

Who is this book for?

This book is for asexual and aromantic folks who have questions about how to navigate relationships of all kinds. Whether we're talking about friendships, romantic relationships, casual dates, or casual intimate partners, this book aims to speak specifically to folks in the ace and aro communities and about the unique challenges we face in these areas.

Let's be clear about what those communities are and who they contain.

Asexual (or "ace") folks are folks who do not or rarely experience sexual attraction. The definition seems simple, but it describes a wide spectrum of experiences and relationships with sex and sexual attraction. Some ace folks don't have sex. Some do. Some never experience sexual attraction. Some do under certain circumstances. Some are comfortable with other forms of physical intimacy. Some aren't. Some enjoy fantasy, kink, or porn. Others don't. There is no universal asexual experience, but across the spectrum of aceness, folks are experiencing sexual attraction in a way that goes against cultural and societal expectations.

Aromantic (or "aro") folks are folks who do not or rarely experience romantic attraction. This is another simple definition that belies a more complex and nuanced set of experiences. Some aro folks pursue romantic relationships. Some focus on other relationship structures that don't include romance. Some don't pursue relationships at all. Some aro folks enjoy romantic stories and media. Others do not. Some express and experience love in non-romantic contexts. Some don't experience love in any context. As in the asexual experience, there is no universal aromantic experience. Aromanticism includes the entire community of people whose experience of romance lies outside the bounds of our cultural and societal romantic expectations.

Some folks situate their experience in both of these communities, inhabiting lives that are asexual and aromantic. Aroace folks are folks whose experiences of both sexual and romantic attraction go against our cultural and societal expectations. While some aroace folks will adopt behaviors and relationships that align with cultural norms, others will construct their own relationship forms or simply knit together networks of community that aren't focused on traditional romantic and sexual relationships. The aroace experience is as diverse and varied as asexual and aromantic experiences are individually. There's no monolithic aroace experience.

This book is written to speak directly to the folks in these communities. Ace, aro, and aroace folks face challenges in relationships that allosexual and alloromantic folks (folks who do experience sexual or romantic attraction in culturally expected ways) do not. We rarely ever see our relationships centered, and we never see this kind of resource designed to speak directly to us.

This book is also written to speak to young adult readers, although anyone of any age can find things in this book that are helpful. But this book will be particularly useful to folks who are at the beginning of their journey or early in their exploration of how their ace or aro identities fit into their goals and aspirations for relationships.

If you're here and not on the ace or aro spectrums, stick around! I'm glad you're here, too. Good relationships are good relationships no matter the sexual and romantic orientations of the people in them. I hope you'll take what's offered here as an opportunity to learn more about us and how we build relationships. (Spoiler: It'll look more familiar than you might assume.) You may find that the relationship skills, advice, and strategies here are just as useful to you as they are to ace, aro, and aroace folks.

A quick note on terms

Throughout the book, we'll be speaking about ace and aro folks in a few different configurations.

Sometimes, we'll just be talking about the asexual experience. In those cases, we'll just use "ace" or "asexual" to note who we're talking about. Sometimes, we'll just be talking about the aromantic experience. In those cases, we'll just use "aro" or "aromantic" to note who we're talking about. When we're talking about folks who inhabit both experiences, we'll refer to those folks as "aroace."

When we need to speak of these two communities and the overlaps between them in a broader sense, we'll use the term "aspec." Aspec refers to the broad spectrum of individuals who exist on either the ace or aro spectrum, or on both. Aspec not only acknowledges that there are resonances and similarities between the ace and aro experiences, but it also highlights that ace and aro folks brush up against similar and related cultural forces.

What is this book trying to do?

My goal here is simple: I want every ace and aro person out there to feel equipped and empowered to pursue the relationships they want. It doesn't matter what kind of relationship that is. It only matters that you know you can ask for it, build it, and be part of making it thrive without compromising who you are.

To that end, this book is divided into two parts.

In the first part—The Relationship Toolbox—we'll look at what it means to be ace and aro in an allosexual world, and we will examine some of the social and cultural forces shaping the way aspec people are treated in the contexts of love and sex. We'll also take a look at the building blocks of good relationships, and we'll talk about those things through an aspec lens.

In the second part—The Relationship Workshop—we'll look at different kinds of relationships through an aspec lens. We'll explore the challenges of beginning relationships of all kinds. We'll look at the ways we can nurture and grow the different kinds of relationships we seek. And we'll talk about how to end relationships in a healthy way.

How can I use this book?

You can think of this book as a handbook of sorts, an operation manual for ace and aro relationships. The focus of this book is practical: definitions, advice, tips, strategies. We'll toss some Big Ideas around (in ways that are approachable, of course), but the goal here is not for this book to help you *think* about the relationships in your life. The goal is for you to *do*: make choices, pursue relationships, nurture healthy bonds, work through problems, and build the kind of human networks that sustain and enrich you. Our lives are less fun when they're strictly theoretical. Lives are meant to be lived.

While there is a Big Story that the entire book is aiming to tell about ace and aro relationships, each chapter can be read as its own world, answering a specific set of questions about a specific stage in or type of a relationship. They can be read out of order. You can breeze past chapters that discuss relationships you don't pursue. The chapters are puzzle pieces you can put together in whatever way creates the best picture for you.

Each chapter is broken down into mini-essays, so it's easy to find what you're looking for. Jump to the parts that are relevant to you. Skip the parts that aren't.

Most chapters conclude with a "Reflect and Act" section in case you want to continue exploring the chapter's ideas. These sections will provide a prompt to reflect on the ideas presented paired with an action you can take to implement the ideas. Sometimes, I'll only include a Reflect prompt, because the work of those sections is primarily internal. Occasionally, these sections will occur within chapters to help you focus on certain concepts or tools. And the book concludes with a resource guide that will point you in a variety of new directions for further inquiry.

Why do we need a book like this?

Too often as ace and aro folks, we are asked to change ourselves in order to be worthy of connection. Whatever we seek—romance, love, companionship, sex, friendship, community—is dangled in front of us like a carrot on a stick while we're told, "Sure, you can have what you want. Just be different. Just be something other than you."

Some of us have sex we don't really want to have. Some of us ascribe to romantic scripts and routines we don't really want to be a part of. Some of us settle for traditional relationships and forgo pursuing the nontraditional relationship structures that are the desires of our hearts. And some of us build relationships when we'd rather move through life without them at all.

Being in fulfilling relationships with others should not come at the cost of ourselves. Our ace and aro identities should not be seen as liabilities in a relationship. They are not obstacles our relationship partners must overlook or overcome. As ace and aro people, we deserve to exist within healthy, positive relationships that affirm who we are and how we experience the world. And, by extension, we deserve to see media reflecting a world that includes those kinds of relationships.

In the long history of relationship writing (and, friend, there is a *lot* of relationship writing out there), very little acknowledges the kinds of relationships aspec folks form and prize. This book aims to change that. As you embark on the journey of bringing your asexuality or aromanticism to prospective partners, you deserve a resource that speaks directly to you and the kinds of bonds you wish to form.

Where this book and I are limited

This book is exploring relationships, asexuality, and aromanticism in broad terms, in order to be a useful resource to as many aspec people as possible. This leads to three things I want to address upfront.

First, this book doesn't account for all the intersections that exist between our aspec identities and the other identities we inhabit. Our experiences of race, gender, ability, class, religion, and the like have profound implications for the way we experience our aspec identities and, in turn, impact the way we exist as ace and aro people within our relationships. The broad view here is not meant to imply that these intersecting experiences do not exist or aren't important. They are. The broad view is only meant to provide a foundational conversation about aspec identity and relationships that is useful in some way to as many people as possible.

Second, this book contains the biases and experiences around relationships that I hold as a white, agender, asexual homoromantic person. This book was written with a Western (particularly a United States-centered) perspective of relationships, because that's the experience I know most intimately. So what's contained here might not apply to everyone who picks up this book. I have attempted to cover and explore concepts that might transcend some of those differences, but that won't be universally true. Know that if some part of this book fails to speak to some truth in your personal or cultural experience, it's a failure of the book and of me. Not of you.

Third, the ace and aro communities are constantly evolving the ways in which they understand and articulate their experiences. Language moves fast in aspec circles. And the ways in which we express and communicate what it means to be ace or aro are always in flux. The understandings contained in this book may not always reflect the most current understandings of aspec experience. They reflect what's true and available at the time I'm writing this. Trust the collective knowledge of the community when it conflicts with what's here in this book.

What we're talking about when we say "relationships"

When we talk about "relationships," the assumption is almost always that we're talking about *romantic* relationships, particularly the kind that's limited to two people, never includes an option for more, and tends to be very heterosexual. And it is also assumed that those exclusive romantic relationships will include sex.

But "relationship" implies so much more than that single kind of partnered connection. There are many forms a relationship can take, and there are many different kinds of connections and intimacies that can be shared between the people in those relationships. Sex and romance are not the only things that define or constitute a relationship.

Throughout this book, we'll talk about "relationships," and we will be talking about them in the broadest of senses. We'll be considering all forms of relationships—from the most intimate and personal we have to the relationships we have with our communities and larger worlds—and we'll be considering them all to have the same weight, the same importance, the same validity, and the same gravity as any other.

Throughout this book, we'll talk about "relationship partners," and we will be talking about them in the broadest of senses. We'll be talking about friends, romantic partners, sexual partners, coworkers, family members, queerplatonic life mates, intentional families. They're all included, and they're all given equal weight and consideration.

Within the pages of this book, no one kind of relationship is supreme. No one kind of relationship is considered ideal. All relationships have a seat at this table. This book is never implying that "relationship" means exclusively paired romantic or sexual connection. "Relationship" here means any meaningful connection we form with other human beings, sometimes in pairs, sometimes in larger units, and sometimes in units so large they encompass people we don't even know halfway across the world.

Now let's get to it.

PART ONE

The Relationship Toolbox

Chapter 1

Ace and Aro in an Allo World

Angelica was my sixth-grade girlfriend.

I met her in band class. She played the flute. I played the trombone. We had a few other classes together, but band was the only class in which I regularly got up the nerve to talk to her. The trombone section left their instrument cases near where the flute section sat, so at the end of every class, when it was time to pack up, I'd find some reason to compliment her while I broke down my trombone.

"You looked like you were really into it during the march section." "I like how you were already in tune during the tune-up." "The flutes were really flutin' today, huh?" It was always a dorky compliment, but Angelica always found it adequate enough to talk to me throughout our walk to the next class.

Eventually, one of those instrument pack-up conversation starters was "Hey, do you want to be my girlfriend?" Thankfully, she said yes, and we were officially taking it to the next level, which meant we *additionally* met up during lunch recess every day and awkwardly stared at the ground while struggling to make small talk.

For Valentine's Day, I decided I wanted to make a grand gesture, something that would demonstrate how seriously I was taking our now-broadening connection. Standard V-Day fare at the time was those Valentine cards that would come in a pack of 30, usually with some cartoon character like He-Man on them saying, "By the power of Grayskull, I LIKE YOU!" It's the thing you got every kid in your class, so while it was a gesture, it was a mostly *empty* gesture. Angelica was my girlfriend. She'd said so herself that one time. She deserved more than a flimsy piece of card stock with maybe G. I. Joe on it making a love pun.

So, on a weekend trip to the mall, en route in our minivan, I told my parents that I needed to make a special purchase.

"I need to get something special for my girlfriend, Angelica, for Valentine's Day," I said.

"We got you those He-Man Valentines already," my mom said.

"Something *special*," I said. "A necklace or something like that. She's my *girlfriend*. And she doesn't even watch He-Man."

"You're in sixth grade, Cody," my mom said with the tone of a raised eyebrow. "What does it mean that she's your 'girlfriend'?"

"She's my *girlfriend*, Mom. We're serious. We're in a committed relationship. You have to do more for the person you're committed to; otherwise, you're not really all that committed, right?"

My mom laughed gently and said, "Honey, you're in sixth grade. We'll help you get her a nice little necklace, but you don't know what the word 'commitment' means yet."

On the one hand, my mom was right. I was 11. I didn't know the first thing about relationships, committed or otherwise. There was nothing in the post-band class or lunch recess conversations with Angelica that even approached the complexity of adult romantic relationships. Except the jewelry.

But in another light, my mom was dead wrong. At 11, I'd absorbed a ton about relationships. I'd learned that the boy should ask the girl out. I'd learned that it was important to give the relationship a title. I'd learned that romantic relationships take precedence over other kinds of relationships, sitting in a higher place of importance and thus deserving special acts and gestures befitting that importance. I'd learned the language of relationships—being "serious" and relationships being "committed"—and the correct ways to deploy that language.

I might not have known how to actually *be* in one, but 11-year-old me sure knew how to fake it.

These instructions about relationships—and specifically about the romance and sex we're supposed to find within relationships—are being instilled in us all the time. Through a powerful and pervasive social osmosis that begins essentially from the time we're born, we are taught very specific "truths" about who we are supposed to be as individuals, what we are supposed to want and desire, how we are expected to pursue those things, and what we are expected to do when we find them. This social osmosis is so pervasive that we often don't even recognize it's happening. But it shapes how we think, how we act, and how we inhabit the different connections we find with other people.

In this chapter, we'll look at the invisible system that's running this social osmosis about relationships, and we'll explore the messages it's sending us. We'll also look at why these messages are so harmful and limiting to aspec people. And we'll consider why, in spite of it all, there's hope.

Normativity

If I asked you to imagine a normal person living a normal life, who and what would you imagine?

If you're imagining from a Western, United States-based perspective, this person you imagine is probably cisgender, displaying all the basic gender cues of the gender you imagine them to have. (While it could go either way, it's more likely you're imagining this person to be a cisgender man.) This person is probably white, definitely not fat, thin but not underweight, without any visible disabilities, and dressed well but conservatively. They probably live in the suburbs in a fairly nice home in a fairly nice neighborhood that is well tended according to shared community values. This person is probably married to a person of the opposite binary gender who is white and cisgender as well. Together, they probably have some white, cisgender kids. This person is emotionally happy, mentally healthy, and probably works a nine-to-five white-collar job that pays them enough money to live this comfortable life.

If you're imagining from other cultures in other parts of the world, the specifics will change, but not the spirit. The family you imagine and the life they lead will most likely reflect the people, environments, and lives that are depicted most often, seen most often, and treated respectfully most often.

But what makes it "normal"? What makes other conditions and outcomes—things like being a different race, being transgender, being queer, being unmarried or in non-monogamous relationships, not having kids, being poor, being disabled, working a blue-collar job or the night shift, living in an apartment or a mobile home, being unhappy, living with mental illness—outside of what we consider "normal"? And what makes, in many cases, those non-"normal" conditions and outcomes undesirable, socially unacceptable, or considered worthy of punishment?

The answer is simple: *normativity*.

Normativity is the tendency of societies, across many different cultures, to decide that certain activities, behaviors, and thoughts are "good" while other activities, behaviors, and thoughts are "bad." These societies then form justifications for *why* those things are either "good" or "bad," framing the "good" as things that are natural and inevitable while framing the "bad" as deviances, failures, or errors.

Normativity is a way for societies to regulate the actions of the people within them and to point people in the direction that maximizes their benefit to society. Normativity takes what is most usual in a society—the most usual experience of gender, the most usual experience of attraction, the most usual relationship structure—and decides it will become the most *expected*, the most *good*, because it is the most usual. And normativity takes what keeps the society running most smoothly and successfully and decides it is the most *natural*, the most *desirable*, because it's the most beneficial.

How does normativity achieve this? Societies create *norms*, the specific rules that govern this system of determining what's "good" or "bad." Norms tell us exactly what qualifies as "good" and "bad," and they provide a roadmap for us to follow in order to remain in the "good." Sometimes these norms are explicit—for example, it's pretty straightforward in most cultures that you shouldn't murder anyone or rob someone's house—but often norms are much harder to see. Instead of being explicit rules, they're woven into the fabric of the world to the point they're basically invisible. We have norms governing everything from the gender that's most desirable to the kind of brain it's best to have to the kind of things it's best you believe, and they're all hidden like code throughout our culture: they show up in our laws, in our stories, in our friends' encouragement, in our parents' expectations, and most powerfully in our own inner voice.

Think of it this way: normativity is a tool societies use to assign *value* to certain behaviors. Behaviors that fall within the norms are endowed with a great deal of value. When you engage in those behaviors, because they are valuable ones, you reap certain benefits. Behaviors that fall outside of the norms are not assigned any value or are assigned negative value. When you engage in those non-normative behaviors (or simply fail to engage in the normative ones), you do not receive any benefits, and, in many cases, receive social and cultural disadvantages.

Norms don't determine something fundamentally true about you or your experience. Norms determine whether or not you and your experience are functionally desired by the society you're in.

Normativity is a large, complex, living system that changes what is "good" and "bad" as the society's needs and concerns change. Norms aren't fixed. As societies change and grow, they require different behaviors and attitudes from their constituents in order to function and thrive. What was normatively desired one hundred years ago isn't necessarily normatively desired now. And what is normatively permissible now may, in the future, suddenly become normatively forbidden.

But the norms that *do* last over many generations—like the ones that govern sex, romance, and relationships—are the ones that become the most hard to see and the most hard to liberate ourselves from.

Normativity and the "Perfect Relationship"

Our cultural ideas about what makes a relationship "good" and "successful" are shaped by norms. And there isn't just one. There's an entire network of norms working to define which relationships have value in a society. Taken all together, that network of norms informs what we think of as the "Perfect Relationship"—the relationship that represents the pinnacle of what we can accomplish in connection with another person, the relationship we should all aspire to create and maintain, the relationship that fully actualizes us and makes us complete human beings.

What does that Perfect Relationship look like?

- The people in it are heterosexual and cisgender.
- The people in it are the only two people in it.
- The people in it are emotionally exclusive (expressed through marriage).
- The people in it are sexually exclusive (expressed through monogamy).
- The people in it are deeply attracted to each other in all ways.
- The people in it remain deeply attracted to each other in all ways forever.
- The people in it produce children through their sexual relationship.

Bonus points if the people in it are white, not disabled, neurotypical, and not part of any other marginalized communities.

What makes this relationship "perfect"? Does it achieve something unique and individual that other relationships don't? Does it provide some deeper connection or more authentic bond than relationships that don't hit these marks? Is there something intrinsically superior about the people who build these kinds of relationships, and do they experience a superior kind of emotional connection with their partner?

No. Of course not. Meeting this handful of arbitrary conditions doesn't make a relationship successful, much less "perfect." These rules simply tick all the normative boxes, making the people who follow them the most useful to society as a whole.

However, the power of this Perfect Relationship myth—and the normative forces that buoy it up—impacts the way we see and pursue all forms of relationships. So we're not just influenced by these norms in our romantic lives. We're feeling the enormous pressure of these norms no matter what kind of relationship we're forming. Prioritize this. Devalue that. Place your energy here. Don't invest yourself there. Commit to this connection. Disregard that connection. Norms are pushing our relationships in a million directions all the time.

There are five normative forces that exert considerable influence on how the Perfect Relationship myth is conceived—allonormativity, compulsory sexuality, amatonormativity, mononormativity, and heteronormativity. Let's look at how these normativities shape the Perfect Relationship myth and focus on how aspec folks experience these forces through their ace and aro identities.

Allonormativity

Allonormativity is the normative cultural force that says all people are allosexual and experience sexual attraction. It insists that sexual attraction is an experience shared by everyone, and that experiencing sexual attraction is a necessary part of one's human experience. Any experiences outside allonormativity—which means all experiences under the asexual umbrella—are considered abnormal, broken, immature, deviant, or simply not fully human.

Allonormativity helps craft the Perfect Relationship myth in a few ways. It insists that relationships cannot be complete without sexual attraction. More than that, it equates the absence of sexual attraction with an absence of love and affection for a partner: if you're not sexually attracted to your partner, how can you be in love with them? Allosexuality also reinforces the centrality and necessity of sex in relationships by asserting sexual attraction's universality. "You're going to experience sexual attraction because you're human," allonormativity says, "and the only natural expression of that, with your perfect partner, is sex."

For asexual folks, these ideas and expectations are crushingly invalidating. Some of us never experience sexual attraction for anyone. Some of us rarely do or do so at extremely low intensities. But all people on the asexual spectrum have a relationship to sexual attraction that lies outside of the demands of allonormativity. In that space, outside of that norm, we are told that, by our nature, we are excluded from the Perfect Relationship, and therefore any relationship we build will be inferior, will be malfunctioning, or will fail.

Compulsory sexuality

Compulsory sexuality, a concept which plays with and expands on the concept of compulsory heterosexuality, is the normative cultural force that says everyone desires and will seek out frequent sex. If you're a person, compulsory sexuality insists, sex is an important part of your life. Not having sex and not wanting sex—which includes many people under the asexual spectrum—is a sign that something is fundamentally wrong within a person, that some deficiency exists, or that a person has simply not matured in the appropriate ways.

How does compulsory sexuality help construct the Perfect Relationship myth? Compulsory sexuality insists that to be a healthy, complete person in a healthy, complete relationship, sex must be a part of it. It also underpins the social insistence that real, strong, true relationships will eventually produce children through the sex that's inevitable between people who love each other. Compulsory sexuality, along with allonormativity, not only makes sex an end goal of pursuing relationships, but makes sex and sexual attraction a necessary ingredient to validate those relationships, to make those relationships real. Without sex and sexual attraction, these two normative forces claim, relationships aren't whole, aren't functioning, and aren't *real*.

Compulsory sexuality excludes folks all along the asexual spectrum. For ace folks who choose not to include sex in their lives, compulsory sexuality is an accusation of brokenness. Their choice to not have sex marks them as immature, insufficient, and incomplete. For ace folks who do include sex in their lives, compulsory sexuality is there to say, "That's not good enough." Whether it's not wanting it enough, not wanting it for the right reasons, or not wanting it in the "correct" ways, asexual folks who have sex remain outside compulsory sexuality's conventions.

Amatonormativity

Amatonormativity, a concept coined by philosopher Elizabeth Brake, is the normative cultural force that insists everyone thrives in exclusive romantic relationships. It assumes that romantic attraction is a universal human experience and that romantic relationships are an essential ingredient in each of us reaching our fullest potential. If you don't want romantic relationships or don't experience romantic attraction, amatonormativity insists, you're living a stunted life. You're missing out on something fundamental that everyone else feels and understands, something that makes them complete human beings.

Amatonormativity shapes the Perfect Relationship myth by centralizing the importance of romantic connection. How can a relationship be perfect unless it contains one of the elements essential to human experience? By casting romance as a key that unlocks human completeness, amatonormativity locks all relationship success in the box of romantic love.

But amatonormativity makes a further insistence. It also insists on exclusivity. It says that romance must be exclusive in order to be truly fulfilling and valuable. We have to fall in love, and we have to fall in love with *one person and one person only* in order to be our fullest selves. Not only does this prevent us from feeling romantic love for more than one person, but it diminishes the importance of other kinds of relationships once we've found The One.

Amatonormativity denies the basic humanity of aromantic folks. It excludes aro folks from what it considers a full and complete human, and it minimizes the value and importance of the kinds of relationships many aro folks center in their lives: close friendships, platonic life partnerships, queerplatonic relationships, and other nontraditional human networks. Amatonormativity dismisses these relationships out of hand and demands aro folks be cast aside when alloromantic folks find romantic partners.

Mononormativity

Mononormativity, coined by Marianne Pieper and Robin Bauer, is the normative cultural force that says exclusivity, both emotional and sexual, is the natural and necessary way to pursue romantic relationships. Mononormativity puts all the eggs in one basket. It's *serious* about exclusivity. If you're seeking out multiple people to fulfill your emotional and sexual needs, mononormativity says you're in flawed, inadequate relationships. And because mononormativity is so jazzed about being exclusive, it also demands that you find all the things you want in one person.

Mononormativity plays an important role in the Perfect Relationship myth. First, it is the driving force behind our idea of there being The One, that magical single person who activates all of our attractions and meets all of our needs. They're out there, mononormativity says, so hold out until you find them. It also grounds the way we sort relationships into a hierarchy, with those exclusive romantic and sexual relationships at the top and platonic relationships at the bottom. Mononormativity pushes us to seek out and prioritize the one relationship that does all the things, thereby encouraging us to push aside any relationship that fails to do it all.

Aspec folks are hurt by mononormativity in two key ways. First, many aspec folks will seek out nontraditional relationship structures like polyamory, ethical non-monogamy, queerplatonic relationships, and the like as the best expressions of their identities. These relationships, under mononormativity, are culturally shamed and devalued. And aspec folks are harmed by the way mononormativity works on other people. Because others are seeking The One, that perfect person who meets all the needs and does all the things, many aspec people are seen, because of our ace or aro identities, as inadequate for the job. We're dismissed as relationship prospects because we don't meet the needs of mononormativity. Further, the successful platonic relationships we build, like our powerful friendships, are often summarily cast aside by others in favor of their sexual and romantic ones.

Heteronormativity

Heteronormativity, a term popularized by social theorist Michael Warner, is the normative cultural force that assumes every person is heterosexual by default and that any orientation that deviates from heterosexuality is fundamentally unnatural. Those deviations are attributed to someone's choice (usually immoral or deviant) or from some kind of defect or illness. Heteronormativity assumes that man–woman pairings are the only kind of sexual and romantic pairings we are built to pursue and occupy. It denies natural variation in human sexuality. Heteronormativity also insists that the people in these pairings adhere to traditional gender roles—men behaving like "men," and women behaving like "women"—and to rules about sexual and romantic exclusivity. There is also the expectation that heteronormative pairings will produce children, and those children will be raised to follow the same heteronormative rules that created them.

Heteronormativity leverages the other normativities—allonormativity, compulsory sexuality, mononormativity, and amatonormativity—and crafts a definitive ideal for human relationships. It not only dictates what can be done within the Perfect Relationship, but it also dictates who can be in them. It restricts these benchmarks for full personhood to those who desire the "correct" gendered partner and those who, themselves, perform gender in a traditionally accepted way.

Merely existing as an aspec person defies heteronormativity. But the box heteronormativity creates around what makes a relationship worthwhile is so rigid and so small that aspec folks are almost always forced to give up parts of themselves to inhabit any relationship heteronormativity approves of. The kinds of relationships that center the way ace and aro folks experience the world are wholesale excluded by heteronormativity, so the ace or aro person is always faced with an impossible choice: compromise something to fit into the box or go without.

Normative forces and intersectionality

We've talked about these five normative forces—allonormativity, compulsory sexuality, amatonormativity, mononormativity, and heteronormativity—in very broad terms. This is useful, in order to get a basic sense of how these forces work. But that broadness creates a narrow kind of understanding. We've discussed them as they might impact a generic aspec person in the world.

And that's the problem. There is no generic aspec person. Asexuality and aromanticism are one facet of a person's experience. They are one identity among many that a person may inhabit. All of the other identities we can inhabit while we inhabit asexuality and aromanticism—race, gender, class, disability, religion, neurotype, and the like—can impact the way we experience them and the normative forces that work on them.

This is called *intersectionality*. It's a framework coined by law professor Kimberlé Crenshaw. Intersectionality is a way of looking at an individual's intersecting identities and how those intersections impact that individual's experience of oppression. We can be disadvantaged across multiple identities, intersectionality argues, so understanding how those intersections compound oppression or alleviate oppression is important to truly understanding a person's experience of the world.

How we move through the world outside of our aspec identities—our race, our gender, our class, our religion, whether or not we are disabled, whether or not we are neurodivergent, etc.—will change not only the way we experience our aspec identity but the way we experience the normative forces that surround them. For example, Black femme aspecs will experience compulsory sexuality differently from white male aspecs, because Black femmes experience a racialized hypersexualization that white men do not. Nonbinary and trans aspecs will feel different pressures from heteronormativity than their cisgender counterparts due to the different ways they inhabit and express their gender. Disabled aspecs may experience a magnified marginalization from allonormativity because society judges their bodies through both of those experiences at once. Some of our identities intensify the negative impacts of normativity. Some of our identities will lessen the negative impacts.

When we think about these normative forces and their impacts on aspec folks—as well as basically everything in this book about relationships—it's important to remember that the whole of who we are needs to be accounted for. We each live our lives through a series of lenses, and each lens has its own unique way of changing our view. When the lenses magnify the harm, we are mindful to care for all of the affected identities. When the lenses lessen the harm, we are mindful of the privilege it bestows on us and try to leverage it to help others.

The Relationship Escalator

The *Relationship Escalator* is an idea coined by writer Amy Gahran. It describes the journey we are expected to take toward a permanently monogamous (both sexually and romantically) cohabitating relationship that is preferably made legitimate through civil or religious marriage.

What does that mean without all the fuss? We're all expected to go from single humans to "forever in love with The One," and there's a clear-cut set of steps and milestones for us to follow to get there.

Follow some other path—*any* other path—and you're not living up to your full potential.

The Relationship Escalator reinforces all of the normative expectations we've discussed so far, but adds a new layer to the mix: a hierarchy of relationship types. The Relationship Escalator focuses on *progress*, on taking steps up the ladder, always moving toward the relationship it considers the ideal. Relationships are valued by how closely they resemble that ideal, and how close they get us to the top of the ladder. In this view, there is an ideal relationship and there are other relationships that we must move beyond and progress through in order to get to the ideal relationship.

If the Relationship Escalator reflected even a smidgen of truth in human experience, ace and aro folks would forever be excluded from reaching their full potential and living complete lives. All that we are and all the ways we form connections with people that contain nontraditional experiences of sexual and romantic attraction are considered inferior on the Relationship Escalator. Friendships? We have to leave those behind. Casual partners? Nope, not serious enough. Sexless relationships? They're inadequate. Loveless relationships? Don't bother. Queer relationships, polyamorous relationships, queerplatonic relationships, intentional families—all of them are unacceptable detours on the Relationship Escalator.

What am I supposed to do with all of this?

It seems a little hopeless, right? It is as though practically everything we're taught about relationships, from the moment we're born, is conspiring against us as aspec people. There's an ideal relationship our culture has decided upon that we can't inhabit without compromising ourselves. There are persistent normative forces reinforcing that ideal and influencing everyone and everything around us to push us to conform. And there's a powerful social script ensuring that all of our relationship alternatives are considered inferior and inadequate.

There's just no hope, right?

Not quite.

Being ace and aro in an allo world means we have to be *aware* of these exclusionary forces and ideas. But we don't have to abide by them. We can do what queer people have been doing since queer people have existed: imagine something different for ourselves and make that imagining real.

It may be hopeless to attempt the creation of aspec-affirming relationships within the confines of these social norms and scripts. But there is great potential—amazing *possibility*—if we decide to construct those aspec-affirming relationships in a space of our own, a space that rejects norms, that eschews social scripts, that believes in a broader, more varied range of relationship forms and structures.

And that's what we're going to do from here on out. We're going to keep these normative Big Baddies in the back of our mind—because the devil you know beats the devil you don't—but they won't inform the way we imagine awesome relationships. Instead, we're going to start from scratch and build relationship norms and relationship skills from the ground up.

And they're going to celebrate—not negate—our authentic aspec selves.

Reflect and Act

Reflect: For each of the normativities discussed—allonormativity, compulsory sexuality, amatonormativity, mononormativity, heteronormativity—and the Relationship Escalator, think about the ways they show up in your life. Where do you see these ideas represented? Who in your life reinforces these ideas?

Act: Have a conversation with someone in your life about one of these normative forces. Define it. Share examples. Share how it shows up in your life. Share its impact. Ask them where they see this normative force in their life and whether or not it impacts their relationships. Making people aware of normative forces and how they work can make them more empathetic and supportive of lives and experiences that are outside norms—like asexuality and aromanticism.

Chapter 2

A New Kind of Perfect

In college, I studied theater to become an actor. I loved being on stage, and I was hungry—voracious, really—to make my life and career in plays and musicals. And I was dreaming big. My ambition was, as drunkenly stated in a home video made by a friend at a cast party during my freshman year, to "have three Tonys by the time I'm 30 and be more famous than *any* of you!"

My acting ambitions clearly didn't pan out—official Tony count: zero—but there are many lessons I learned during my time as a budding thespian that help me in the work I do today. A favorite lesson, and one that's useful to the matter at hand, came from a wonderful man named Richard.

In my sophomore year, I was cast in a production of the musical *Hair* as the Tourist Lady. The Tourist Lady has one scene and one short song, but it's a standout moment. It's a drag part, and the song's a hoot, allowing me to show off a falsetto range that flirted with the vibes of operetta. It's also the kind of acting part I love: one big flashy moment in the show that was totally memorable, then a relaxing time as a no-name ensemble member for the rest of the show.

Richard was our vocal director, teaching us the score and leading us through the intricacies of each of our vocal parts. Richard was one of the most fabulous men I've ever met. Ridiculously talented and so generously in love with the art of making theater, he could effortlessly transform any situation into a revelatory teaching moment. With a wry smile and a flourish of a hand gesture, Richard could turn an explanation of how to tackle a vocal phrase into a moment that would mindbend you into a new way of seeing the world.

During a one-on-one rehearsal of my song, I was getting frustrated over one of the higher passages, a lengthy held note which was designed to be a crowd-pleasing vocal flex. I couldn't sustain it, or if I did sustain it, the note would sound funky or veer a little flat.

"What exactly is frustrating you right now?" Richard asked after I'd blown the moment for the twentieth time and grunted my dissatisfaction.

"I'm frustrated because I can't get this right," I said. "It's my big moment in the show, and I want it to be perfect. And if I can't hit it perfectly, then what's the point?"

"There's nothing more boring to me than perfect," he said. "Perfect is the end. You perform the song perfectly—then what? What's discoverable? What's unexpected? What's *possible*?" He took his pencil and pointed the eraser end at me. "I'd rather you give me some imperfect version of this song that makes me feel that you're alive, that I'm alive, so I can look forward to the surprise of what you might do next."

The pencil retracted and a smile snuck across his face. "Let's see what happens if you just aim for the best you've got right now."

After that rehearsal, I stopped aiming for perfection. And every night of the show's run, something different happened during the song. Sometimes I had to take a breath midway through the long-held note. Sometimes the notes would be pitchy. Sometimes I'd mangle the words a little. One night, a surprise and improvised interaction with another actor led to a great discovery and a really funny bit we kept in the show for the rest of the run. There was room to grow and change and discover.

It was never perfect. But it was always *alive*.

Richard is gone now, but any time my brain starts yelling at me to "make it perfect" or "aim for perfection," I remember what Richard taught me that day. Perfect is a constraint. Perfect stops us from growing.

Perfect is always going to keep you from loving what you've got.

Why we need to abandon the Perfect Relationship myth

Why does the normative Perfect Relationship myth fail most people?

It is obsessed with what gender you are, how you inhabit that gender, how you want sex, who you want for sex, how you want romance and love, who you want for romance and love, and how limited and focused you can make that pursuit. It is worried about what your relationship can produce or sustain. It perceives you as a product in need of an appropriate box, and your value rests not on who and what you are, but how closely you can mold yourself to some culturally defined default.

In the Perfect Relationship, "perfect" is a straitjacket. It puts limits on the ways we can understand and express our identities. It puts constraints on the ways in which we can share our affection, love, and intimacy with other people.

We can do better than that, right? We can imagine something more expansive, more inclusive. We can dream up a set of relationship values that focus on what is possible for people to build together: what keeps them safe, what encourages them to grow, what allows them to be the fullest version of themselves.

We can imagine relationships that don't work to deny or erase ace and aro people, but instead embrace and celebrate who we are. Furthermore, we can imagine relationships that uplift aspec folks while still affording allo folks the same space and support. These are relationships that meet us where we are, wherever on the spectrum of human experience that may be.

A new kind of "perfect"

We're going to ditch the idea of any relationship being "perfect"—as Richard taught us, the pursuit of perfection is the enemy of most things—and we are going to focus on a relationship structure that supports and celebrates us as whole aspec people. Instead of building our ideal relationship on normative constructs and arbitrary notions of what's "right" and "wrong" in human experience, we're going to focus on skills and ideas that make no judgments and consider our aspec identities and experiences worthy of respect.

Our "New Kind of Perfect" focuses on four core beliefs:

1. Romance and sex do not make a relationship real, valid, or valuable. They can be *part* of what people want and pursue in a relationship, but they are not essential to a relationship working or to a relationship *mattering*.

2. The outcomes of a relationship—whether it ends in marriage or produces children, for example—do not make a relationship real, valid, or valuable. They can be part of what people want and pursue in a relationship, but they are not essential to a relationship working or to a relationship *mattering*.

3. Hierarchies do not make a relationship real, valid, or valuable. We do not need to devalue or dismiss one kind of relationship in order to make another kind feel important. All relationship types are whole and worthy of prioritizing within themselves.

4. What makes a relationship real, valid, and valuable is determined by the people in the relationship, collaboratively and consensually. No relationship built with respect and care for the wholeness of the people in it should be seen as broken, wrong, or lacking.

Think of the possibilities this opens up for us. We're no longer governed by oppressive norms telling us who and what we have to be in order to be seen as worthy. Whether or not we provide the correct amounts of romance and sex does not determine our worth or the worth of the relationships we're in. We're no longer focused on what our relationships produce, but rather on the experience we have within them. And we aren't trying to slot our relationships into a hierarchy someone else decided upon, but rather we're giving every valued connection in our lives the weight and importance we want to give it. *We* are deciding what works *for us*, and as long as what we build is supportive of us and our relationship partners, it is good and right and valuable. We have space to live in all of our complexities. We have room to evolve our understanding of those complexities. We have room to learn, to change, to grow.

It's the kind of thing Richard would wholeheartedly approve of.

The Relationship Toolbox for "A New Kind of Perfect"

Our normative Big Baddies—allonormativity, amatonormativity, heteronormativity, mononormativity, compulsory sexuality, and the Relationship Escalator—make up the tool box for the Perfect Relationship myth. But what's in the tool box for our "A New Kind of Perfect" relationship?

While it takes a lot to build any successful relationship—and every relationship requires its own special blend of components to make it work—there are ten basic tools we can turn to in order to achieve the goals of our more expansive vision for relationships. They are autonomy, consent, boundaries, communication, commitment, compromise, trust, respect, recognition, and care.

None of these tools are new, unheard of, or revelatory. Many of them are as obvious as breathing, and we are assumed to already know how to ask for, receive, and provide these things. But because there is so little conversation about ace and aro lives in our culture, there are never conversations about these relationship tools as they apply to aspec lives.

Are these tools useful to everyone? Certainly. They speak to needs in allo–allo relationships as well as those with aspec folks in them. But we'll look at these tools as they relate to aspec folks in particular, focusing on how these tools support and center our particular experiences within relationships.

While the next few chapters will explore these ten tools in more depth, we'll introduce them here and learn a little of why they're important to aspec folks.

Autonomy

Autonomy is the ability to make decisions for ourselves, ideally when those decisions line up with our personal values.

Autonomy is not just being able to make decisions for ourselves about what we do with our bodies in relation to other people. That's an important part of it, to be sure. But it's also about our ability to make those decisions as a reflection of our own interests, our own values.

Autonomy is very important for aspec folks in relationships, because so much of the cultural and normative messaging we get often demands we do things we don't want to do: have sex, accept romance, have looser physical and emotional boundaries. Understanding and being able to exert our autonomy helps us protect our aspec selves.

Consent

Consent is when we freely and voluntarily agree to the wishes, desires, or proposals of another person. Often consent is talked about in the context of sexual activity, but consent can apply to many different situations in a relationship.

Consent is powerful. When we can give consent freely and voluntarily, we are exercising our control over our body and the freedom we have to choose what we do. When we are unable to consent or when our consent is taken from us, we are stripped of our power to preside over our body and mind. Consent is a way we physicalize our right to determine how we exist in the world.

This authority is so crucial for aspec people. In a world that refuses the things we want for our bodies and minds, being able to exercise consent is essential in living our aspec lives fully and authentically. We need to be able to control when we say "yes." We need to be able to control when we say "no." Consent is key.

Boundaries

Boundaries are the limits we set for ourselves in relationships in order to keep us safe and healthy.

Boundaries help us make decisions in complicated situations. They protect us when situations become challenging or unsafe, and they help us build spaces with our relationship partners that support our wellbeing.

Because our needs and wants as aspec folks often fall outside what's expected by normative relationships, being able to set boundaries, negotiate them with a partner, and put them into action helps us build aspec-affirming relationships.

Communication

Communication is the process where relationship partners share thoughts, feelings, and experiences that are important and work to reach mutual understanding of those thoughts, feelings, and experiences.

Communication isn't just talking. It's deeper than that. Successful communication is about reaching a place of *understanding*, a place where both you and your partner feel seen. It's a process—sometimes it takes a while to reach that place of understanding—but communication has to be something you do together, reaching for mutual clarity and understanding.

Good communication is so important for aspec folks and our relationship partners. So much of our experience is rendered invisible, misunderstood, or intentionally mischaracterized by the outside world.

Good communication is the space we make to correct those harms and to assert what's true about us and our community.

Commitment

Commitment is a mutual agreement between you and your partner to work together to achieve shared goals or live shared values.

Commitment comes in all sizes and all scales of importance. It doesn't have to look like promises to be together forever or pledges of your eternal fidelity. It doesn't have to be focused on long-term plans. It doesn't have to include exclusivity. It doesn't have to look like anything specific at all. All commitment requires is a shared vision of what your relationship will look like and how it will function, as well as a shared focus on building that *together*.

Commitment is important for aspec folks in their relationships. A lot of what people choose in their relationships is based on social expectations. We do what we think we're expected to do. So commitment becomes a tool for aspec folks to reset those expectations and to ground our relationships in ace- or aro-affirming agreements.

Compromise

Compromise is a process of reaching agreement with your relationship partner through mutual give-and-take. It's a way to honor our differences and uniquenesses while making room for those of our relationship partner.

Compromise is tough because it's not always easy to know when it's healthy. Sometimes our partners can ask us to compromise in ways that diminish us. Society can ask us to compromise in ways that make us betray our values. But healthy compromise—the kind that strikes a balance between two different sets of needs, wants, and experiences—is a powerful tool in relationships.

Being really good at compromise is a useful tool for aspec folks. It's important for us to have control and confidence over what we agree to engage in with our partners when our needs and wants don't align.

And it's equally important for us to know when compromise isn't the right decision, when compromise takes us too far away from who we are and what we value.

Trust

Trust is feeling we can rely on another person because they make us feel safe. When we trust someone, we feel confident that they will not hurt or violate us.

There are several ways we can build trust with our partners. And there are ways to rebuild trust when it's been broken. We can think of trust as the soft place we can land when relationships ask us to do hard things. Trust makes the personal risk of relationships easier.

Being aspec in relationships can ask a lot of us. It requires a high degree of vulnerability and bravery to ask for the things we want, to say no to the things we don't, and to negotiate terms for relationships that sit outside the comfortable norms others lean on. Trust in our partner— and in ourselves and our own capacity—can give us an extra boost to make it through those challenges.

Respect

Respect is when we hold someone else's feelings, wishes, beliefs, and experiences as valid and *theirs*, and we do not interfere with or devalue those feelings, wishes, beliefs, and experiences.

Respect is as much an action as it is an attitude or state of mind. When we treat others with respect, we not only acknowledge their differences and individual experiences, but we hold space for them to live and thrive in those differences and experiences. Respect is also not a one-way street. We can—and *should*—also extend respect inward, to ourselves. Self-respect is enormously important not only in building positive relationships but in becoming the best people we can be.

For aspec folks, learning how to ask for and receive respect within our relationships, particularly in those relationships we have with folks outside of our communities, is a pivotal skill. So often, the world asks us to accept less than respect and to afford ourselves less than respect.

We can grow to expect a respect-less existence. But we deserve respect for our aspec identities from every relationship partner, no matter the configuration.

Recognition

Recognition is the feeling of being seen, fully, for who you are by another person. It is the feeling that a relationship partner understands the basic parts that make us up and sees those things without judgment.

Recognition is a powerful and validating thing. It's something we seek from relationships of all kinds. We want people to see us. We want to feel known by the people we share space and experience with. Recognition makes vulnerability and authenticity easier. And it is also a powerful gift we can give other people. When we see others fully—when we create a space where they feel understood and validated—they feel free to share their full, best selves with us.

For ace and aro folks—and, honestly, for all marginalized folks—recognition takes on deeper meaning. We already move through a world that refuses to see us. Social norms render us invisible. Laws render us invisible. Racism, homophobia, transphobia, misogyny, aphobia, ableism, and the like render us invisible. Being seen in our fullness by a relationship partner reminds us we are not invisible. We take up space in the world—a space we deserve—and we are enough.

Care

Care is the practice of extending ourselves in the pursuit of providing for the health, welfare, and protection of someone else. Care is the choice to use our resources, in all meanings of the word, to attend to the needs of someone else. Care can exist despite a person's emotional proximity to us. We can provide care for those who are the closest to us. We can also provide care for those we don't even know. But a strong relationship will include care, in mutual exchange.

Care, like respect, can also be focused inward. Self-care—the practice of using our resources to provide for our own health, welfare, and protection—is important. We don't have to wait for others to provide care for us. We can often provide it for ourselves.

It is important to note the use of the word "practice" here. Care is *active*. It is a thing we *do*. Care consists of actions, and even though they're predicated on feelings like respect and recognition, we aren't providing care unless we're engaged in some form of doing. (We'll talk more about what this "doing" looks like in Chapter 5.)

Care is a powerful, transformative tool. For aspec folks, it can be the protective barrier that shields us from the harshness of an aphobic world. It can heal us and rejuvenate us. And care is also something we can use to heal and rejuvenate the communities and world around us. Care is a critical component of building healthy relationships at all scales, and it is at the heart of living happily and well in all our various communities and relationships.

How to use the Relationship Toolbox

Throughout the rest of this part of the book, we'll be looking at the individual tools in the Relationship Toolbox and exploring them more deeply. We'll tackle them in small groups, based on the ways the tools interact and the ways we use them.

We'll start with the three tools that help us manage our bodies and our borders: autonomy, consent, and boundaries. Next, we'll explore the three tools that help us manage what we owe each other: commitment, communication, and compromise. And finally, we'll explore the four tools that help us and our relationships thrive: trust, respect, recognition, and care.

Each of these tools could be the subject of their own book, so we'll be focusing on the fundamentals here, as well as the concerns and questions that most impact ace and aro folks. We'll also discuss them broadly, through the lens of multiple relationship types, interchangeably. (In Chapter 6 and beyond, we'll zero in more closely on different relationship types.) So you might not learn everything you need to know about these skills in the next three chapters, but you'll find pathways into these concepts that can ground both exploration and further learning.

Okay, but isn't something missing?

You might be saying to yourself, "That's it? Aren't you missing something? Where's *romance*? Where's *sex*? Aren't those kind of necessary in a relationship?"

No. They're not. The exclusion of romance and sex as part of the Relationship Toolbox is intentional. Sex and romance are not necessary to build strong relationships. Are they often nice? Sure, if that's the kind of thing you're looking for. Do some folks *feel* as though sex and romance are necessary components? Sure, the desire for romance and/or sex can feel as urgent and necessary as breathing for some. But that urgency, that sense of the necessary, isn't a universal experience, nor is it a human default.

Sex and romance do not need to be present in order for a relationship to thrive.

Once you take romance and sex out of the relationship equation, you begin to see what relationships truly are: spaces we build with other human beings that provide mutual support in the journey to be our best selves. And when we can see relationships in that way, we can see that *all* kinds of relationships are able to nurture those spaces. *All* types of relationships can help us reach that goal.

And when *that* becomes the way we see relationships, hierarchies fall away. No single kind of relationship looks more important than another. No single kind of relationship matters more than another. We see every connection for what it is and what it wants to be, instead of seeing a connection in the ways it falls short of perfection.

In rejecting the old way of seeking perfection, we find a new kind of perfect: one that not only honors ace and aro folks in their wholeness, but honors what we can bring to the relationships we build and to the people we choose to build them with.

Reflect and Act

Reflect: Which of the ten relationship tools do you feel is most important? Least important? How would you organize them in terms of their value to you? Which of the ten relationship tools do you feel you live successfully? Which do you live less successfully? How would you organize them in terms of how well you live them in your life currently?

Act: Think of someone in your life who you feel successfully embodies one of these relationship tools. Tell them. Ask them for insight on how they think about or approach that tool. For example, you could say: "Hey, I think you're really good at communicating, and I really appreciate that. Do you have some advice on how to communicate in your style?" Showing our gratitude for good relationship skills is always in order, but conversations like these help us emulate the specific ways we experience good relationship skills.

Chapter 3

Our Bodies and Our Borders

Autonomy, Consent, and Boundaries

Here's an unavoidable fact: everybody's got a body.

We're in a body all day, every day. We move about the world in a body. We experience the textures, tastes, sights, smells, and sounds of everything around us through the features of our body. Our body is the conduit through which we perceive and engage with other bodies, also moving about the world. The whole of our experience relies, in some part, on the fact of—and the *possibilities* of—our bodies.

So it makes sense that the body, what we choose to do with it, and how we choose to protect its borders would be central to healthy relationships. In every context, relationships wither or thrive around questions of the body. Do I have the authority to choose what I do with my body? Do I have the power to control what others do with my body? Can I set boundaries around what makes my body feel safe? Are those boundaries respected by other bodies?

These questions are important for everyone, ace or allo. But for aspec folks, questions about our bodies and our borders are subject to a different kind of gravity. Because our bodies experience sexual and romantic attraction in culturally subversive ways, the choices we are inclined to make about and for our bodies are almost universally condemned by the world around us. And even when we do use our bodies in the normative ways—I'm thinking of sex- and romance-favorable aspec folks here—we may want to set different boundaries and expectations than are assumed by our allo partners. There's more pressure on us to communicate and defend our answers to the questions of the body.

In this chapter, we'll look at the three relationship tools concerning our bodies and their borders—autonomy, consent, and boundaries. These tools not only ensure our safety but also play important roles in protecting and asserting our aspec identities as well.

TOOL #1: AUTONOMY

Autonomy is about our values

Let's begin with autonomy, the ability to make decisions for ourselves, when those decisions line up with our personal set of values. That intersection of decisions and values is important, so it's where we'll begin taking a closer look.

It's easy to think autonomy is just being able to make your decisions and not having someone else make them for you. In some ways, that is autonomy. But while it's correct, it's less than complete. There are many circumstances in which we can make our own decisions but those decisions do not align with what we believe or what we want. We can place the needs of others over our own needs. We can place the wants of others over our own wants. We can make decisions based on societal expectations, on peer or familial pressure, or on negative thoughts or ideas we hold about ourselves. Yes, we're *choosing* to do a thing, but the choice isn't coming from our own best interests.

In all of those situations, we are making our own decisions. But until those decisions line up with our own values—values that *we* hold for *our* wellbeing—we aren't acting *autonomously*. Autonomy is when our actions embody our values, when we are choosing and doing in alignment with what we believe.

So where does autonomy show up in our lives?

A good way for us to get our brains around autonomy is to think about where questions of autonomy show up in our lives. These are the spaces where you will be tasked with making decisions about yourself where it will be important for you to make those decisions according to your values.

Defining ourselves. How do we define ourselves? What are our interests? Where do our passions lie? Our ability to describe and define ourselves is a foundational component of autonomy. Self-definition happens when we say, "I am asexual," or "I am aromantic." But self-definition is much broader than our orientation identity labels. "I am a writer." "I am a pacifist." "I am an activist." "I am a friend." "I am a spiritual person." All of these are ways we self-define. Deciding what ways we self-define and making those decisions from the foundation of what's important to us is exercising our autonomy.

Defining our human networks. Who do we associate with? Whom do we support? Who supports us? Who shares our time and capacity? Our ability to determine and construct human networks for ourselves is another important piece of autonomy. When we find and nurture friendships, join activity groups, select a church, go out on dates, establish family traditions, or develop life partnerships of any kind, we're shaping our human network. Deciding our associations—from the loosest ones to the deepest and most complicated ones—is a fundamental way we assert our autonomy.

Defining our interests, ideas, and opinions. What are we interested in? What are our worldviews? What do we like and dislike? When can we hold on to or change those opinions? Our ability to determine and pursue the interests, ideas, and opinions we hold are an important facet of autonomy. This ranges from the minuscule—what toppings we want on a pizza or whether or not we enjoy horror movies—to the more global and important—what constitutes justice for other human beings, the ways we vote, or the ways we engage in bettering the world. Deciding what interests, ideas, and opinions we hold, as well as deciding the ways we share and pursue those things, is central to exercising our autonomy.

Defining our individual space and time. Who gets to share our personal space? When do we choose to join someone in theirs? What do we do with our time? When do we share our time and when do we take time for ourselves? Our ability to manage our individual space and time is another important way we exercise our autonomy. We should always be in control of who shares our personal space and who receives our time and attention. Beyond that, we should also always be able to determine when we accept or reject requests from others to share their space and time. Our individual time and space are important resources, and when we control how those resources are used by ourselves or others, we're exercising our autonomy.

When taken together, these four areas of autonomy map out the life we choose for ourselves. By knowing, across these four areas, what we want to do, what we want to feel, and what we want to be, we can start to map out what we want to *share* with others. Autonomy is, in many ways, the first step in moving from "me" to "we."

Why is autonomy important to me as an aspec person?

Aspec folks are under a lot of pressure. We are under the constant pressure of society's expectations for the kinds of lives we should lead. We are under pressure from our interpersonal networks which reinforce those societal expectations. And we can feel incredible pressure from the people closest to us—family, best friends, relationship partners—to "just do what everyone else is doing" or to "do what's natural."

We internalize many beliefs and values that have nothing to do with our own. That can lead us down the road of making decisions and taking actions that are *for other people*. And while sometimes this can be an act of compassion, a kindness, or a gesture of altruism, when it comes to our bodies and our hearts, we deserve to center *ourselves* in our decisions and actions.

This is why autonomy is important for aspec folks. Autonomy tells us that what we want to do with our bodies and what we want to do with our hearts and emotions *matters*. Autonomy tells us those things can and *should* be prioritized. Autonomy is what grounds our ability to say, "My relationship with sex and romance is legitimate, and I can ask that it be respected."

Autonomy versus intimacy

Okay, but if we focus so much on who we are apart from other people, how do we develop closeness with our partners?

As with all things, relationships require balance. On one side of this balancing act is autonomy. We have to understand who we are apart from the influence and participation of other people. On the other side of the balancing act is *intimacy*, the connectedness and closeness we develop with other people. Intimacy is about exploring our possibilities with other people. Successful relationships thoughtfully balance the two.

When relationships are starting out, intimacy often takes the lead. The freshness and excitement of new relationships, be they friendships, romantic relationships, or something else, make it easy for us to emphasize intimacy. New relationships make us curious, eager to learn more, hungry to spend time in the good feelings a new connection brings.

We should absolutely enjoy these good feelings. They're good, after all! Of course we should enjoy them. And we should be open to the ways this closeness with others can impact us. Maybe we get turned on to a new hobby or a new interest. Maybe we get the courage to try something we have never tried before. Maybe the intimacy we share with someone new helps us see some part of ourselves in a new way.

This growth and change is good, and we should be open to it, as long as we aren't sacrificing things at the core of who we are. We have to hold both things—the good feelings of intimacy and the grounding strength of autonomy—at once.

Can autonomy ever be a bad thing?

While we should never think of autonomy as a bad thing, we can be thoughtful about how our exercise of autonomy works within our relationships.

Just as we work hard not to abdicate our ability to self-determine and self-govern in our relationships with others, we should also not move too far in the opposite direction. Sometimes we push so hard for our autonomy that we move into a mode of self-isolation, a mode where our desire to protect ourselves and our decisions creates impenetrable walls that keep every kind of connection or support out.

It's easy to understand how we, as ace and aro folks, can enter this mode. Trusting other people is hard. Trusting the world is hard. We get burned time and time again by an allo world telling us we're broken or sick or immature or childish. And we constantly feel the pressure from other people to make different decisions for ourselves—decisions that fit more comfortably into their experience of the world—and to subsume ourselves into the normative expectations of the world.

The inclination to push all of that out is understandable. But it doesn't serve us. Shutting ourselves off from the possibilities of connection with other people is as stifling as diving into connections we lose ourselves in. Yes, rejection sucks. But it shouldn't deter us from sharing what's best about us with people who respect us and celebrate us.

Autonomy red flags

Here are some words and actions to help you identify when a relationship partner isn't respecting your autonomy.

Words: "I didn't say you could do that." "I didn't give you permission to go there." "I don't want you hanging out with them anymore." "No, you don't really like that. You prefer this." "You can't know that about yourself." "I know who you are/what you want better than you do."

Actions: Taking control over where you go and who you spend time with. Trying to change the way you dress or what hobbies you spend time on. Not respecting who you say you are or what you say you experience. Mocking things you like or things you are. Attempts to isolate you from your friends and family.

Reflect and Act

Reflect: Think about the decisions you make in your life—use the four areas we discussed as a guide—and consider which decisions are autonomous, lining up with your values. Which decisions aren't? Why aren't they? If you could change some of those non-autonomous decisions, what would those new decisions look like?

Act: Practice autonomy by taking yourself on an NBM ("Nobody But Me") date. Set aside time to do things you enjoy and choose to do by yourself. Maybe it's dressing up in your favorite outfit and going to a movie of your choice on your own. Or maybe it's a quiet afternoon reading a favorite book and making a lunch that's your favorite. The goal here is to feel what it's like to do things *for* yourself and *with* yourself. Make this a regular practice. It not only helps you gain confidence asserting your autonomy, but it helps you explore your interests and joys on your own terms.

TOOL #2: CONSENT

What is consent?

In the previous section, we discussed the importance of finding a balance between autonomy and intimacy, between making space for ourselves, our wants, our desires, and making space for what we might grow with other people.

Consent is an essential tool in establishing that balance.

Consent is when we freely and voluntarily agree to the wishes, desires, or proposals of another person. Anytime we agree to share some part of ourselves—our body, our emotional capacity, our mental capacity, our resources—we are giving consent. So if we think of autonomy as our way of defining what our wants, needs, values, and desires are for *ourselves*, consent puts autonomy into practice with other people. It's taking what we know about what we want and value and using that knowledge to shape what we experience with others.

Most often, we discuss consent through the lens of sexual activity—and that is an incredibly important kind of consent—but it's important to understand consent exists in all areas of our lives, not just our sex lives. All of the ways in which we share important parts of ourselves with other people require our consent, freely and voluntarily given.

What does it mean when consent is "freely and voluntarily given"?

At its most basic level, consent is saying "yes" to someone's request or desire.

Sounds simple, doesn't it? We say "yes." We participate in whatever we say "yes" to. All is good. Right?

Not really. Nothing in life is ever that cut and dried. And consent, in particular, is more complicated than that. There are many situations in which we might say "yes" to someone's request or desire without making that decision fully autonomously. That's why just saying "yes" isn't enough. We also need to ensure that "yes" comes freely and voluntarily.

Let's explore what that means.

Giving consent freely and voluntarily means giving consent without the pressure of outside forces. We aren't being coerced into giving our consent. We aren't being manipulated into giving our consent. We aren't being forced to give our consent. Our mental and emotional faculties aren't clouded by influences like alcohol, drugs, or heightened emotional distress. Freely and voluntarily given consent comes fully from the person giving it. If pressures from the outside are impacting the decisions we make when saying "yes," our consent isn't given freely. Which means it isn't really our consent.

This is a place where our intersections matter. It's already difficult for ace and aro folks to exercise their consent in an allo world, but it becomes complicated further by ableism, transphobia, racism, and the other systemic forces working on marginalized people. It's harder to exercise your consent as a disabled ace person because systemically your body is treated as not yours in two dimensions. It's harder to exercise your consent as a BIPOC aspec person, because white supremacy already limits the autonomy you're allowed to have. To fully give all aspec individuals the power of consent they deserve, we'll have to continue working against all forms of systemic oppression.

What does consent look like?

Let's look at some key ingredients of freely and voluntarily given consent by identifying some things consent is and isn't.

Consent is...sober. We aren't under the influence of drugs or alcohol. We aren't under the influence of medication that dulls or clouds our capacities. We aren't operating under extreme exhaustion. We aren't operating under extreme mental or emotional distress. We can offer freely and voluntarily given consent when our bodies and minds are at their fullest, clearest capacities.

Consent isn't...coerced or forced. We haven't been asked a thousand times and are just worn down by the asking. We don't believe there will be negative or harmful repercussions if we don't give consent. We aren't being lied to or not given our full set of options. We aren't being threatened with physical or emotional violence. Our resources, our belongings, our safety, our privacy, or our trusted human networks aren't being threatened. We don't consent when consent is forced from us. If someone is exerting pressure on you to change what you are inclined to agree to, you're not freely and voluntarily consenting.

Consent is...specific. We don't give consent to vague, broad categories of things. For example, we don't give consent to "sexual stuff." It's too broad and includes too many things. We consent to specific acts within the broad category and the specific circumstances under which those specific acts take place. "I consent to this specific kind of touch." "I consent to this specific kind of dynamic." "I consent to this specific level of force or intensity." If someone is asking you to generally consent to any broad category of action or experience, you're not freely and voluntarily consenting.

Consent isn't...your silence or their assumptions. Freely and voluntarily given consent is always clearly stated and never assumed. "Well, you didn't say no" is not equal to your consent. "Well, it felt like you were into it" is not equal to your consent. "Well, we talked about this before, so I assumed it was okay" is not equal to your consent. Often, this is called *enthusiastic consent*, which means consent containing the clear presence of a "yes" instead of just the absence of a "no." But we can also think of it as *participatory* or *affirmative consent*, because it requires an active "yes" on our part. If anything is to be assumed around the giving of consent, it is that the answer is assumed "no," until a clear, specific "yes" is given.

Consent is...moment to moment. Consent is given to each request or invitation, in turn. Consenting to one thing does not imply consent to the next thing. And consent is about what's happening here and now. It does not carry over to the same request or invitation a few hours, days, or weeks later. Your consent today does not mean you give consent tomorrow. And our past decisions or actions should never be used by others as a basis for judging the validity of our in-the-moment decisions about consent. Sure, you may have been consenting to certain things in the past, but none of that implies you're being unfair or duplicitous or vengeful if you choose not to consent to those things in the present.

These are just the basics. Consent is a complex and nuanced relationship tool. So don't take this as the definitive word on consent. This is an entry point for you to recognize the moments in which we are requesting and giving consent.

Why is consent important for aspec folks?

As we discussed in Chapter 1, the normative Big Baddies are powerful things, shaping not only the way we think but also the way we *behave*. Normative forces construct expectations not only for being but also for *doing*. So, for example, allonormativity doesn't just set expectations for us to *be* allo within ourselves, but it also expects that we will *act* allo in the relationships we build with others.

For allo folks, this expectation is easy to meet. They're doing what comes naturally to them. But it also sets up a belief that it's what everyone *wants* to do, that there exists a kind of implied consent to the behaviors that meet the normative expectations. "If it's what comes naturally," the assumption goes, "it must mean that everyone is cool with doing it."

This is why thinking about, understanding, and communicating what we consent to and what we don't within our relationships is so important for aspec folks. What we want to be and do most often lies outside of those assumptions and expectations. We may not want sex or romance at all in a relationship. We may want very limited versions of them. We may want to pursue certain kinds of physical and emotional intimacies on different time scales than our peers. Articulating what we consent to and what we don't becomes a crucial tool not only in protecting our autonomy but in preserving the experience of our own aspec identities.

There's also something to be said here about other labels that carry expectations. Sure, things like "allo," "aspec," "straight," and "gay" carry normative expectations. But other labels do, too. Think about "boyfriend" or "girlfriend." There are cultural normative expectations around those words, and they carry expectations of behavior. As aspec folks, we will also inhabit those labels uniquely. We will relate to these terms and their expectations differently, and we will want to construct those roles in aspec-affirming ways. Knowing how to utilize the tool of consent around these expectations is important, as well.

Giving and asking for consent

So how do we talk about consent in our relationships?

Establish a strong foundation. Before you even get to the in-the-moment consent conversations, lay the groundwork for those conversations in other parts of your relationship. Make sure you and your relationship partners are having honest, frank conversations about what you like and what you don't, how different elements of physical and emotional intimacy make you feel, what values you hold around different forms of intimacy, and what your prior experiences have been. All of this shared vulnerability helps you make more informed and empathetic requests, and makes it easier for you both to say "no" when the need arises. This goes for platonic relationships and friendships, too. Remember, intimacy doesn't just mean sex or romance.

Get good at asking questions. To ensure your relationships can navigate the hard negotiations of consent, practice asking for and granting consent in all parts of your relationships. Get good at asking questions. "Can I...?" "May I...?" "Would you like it if I...?" "Is it okay if I...?" Start small. Request consent to go in for a hug, to share some space on the couch, to decide where to grab dinner, or to share some stressful feelings because you need a supportive ear. Making a habit of asking for consent in these lower-stakes situations will make it easier to ask when the situations are stickier. And don't forget, this conversation goes both ways. It isn't just your relationship partner asking permission of you. It's also you asking for what you want from your relationship partner.

Make check-ins important. Make it part of your relationship practice to check in with each other even after initial consent is given. "Are you still okay with...?" "Are you still enjoying...?" "Does this still feel good to you?" It reinforces that consent happens moment to moment, and it empowers you both to speak up when your feelings change—even midway through any kind of experience. We want to build relationships that respect the fact a "yes" can become a "no" at any point in an experience.

Talk about "no." Outside of actual consent conversations, have discussions with your partner about what happens when there's a "no." What happens at that moment? How do you want your partner to respond? How do they want you to respond? Establish a game plan to help you both manage these moments. Also, communicate the feelings you both have around "no" moments. What past experiences are brought up by a "no"? What tough emotions—feeling rejected, feeling inadequate, feeling broken, feeling unfair—are brought up by a "no"? The more you and your partner discuss the emotional landscape around these moments, the more empathetic you'll be to each other through them.

Consent red flags

Here are some words and actions to help you identify when a relationship partner isn't respecting your consent.

Words: "I don't have to ask permission." "I just assumed it was okay." "But we did this last week/the other night, so I just assumed it's fine this time." "I know you said you didn't want to, but you don't really mean that." "I know what you want better than you do sometimes." "You're just scared/nervous/unsure. You really want to do this."

Actions: Continuing to do something after you've said no. Persisting in asking after you've said no. Exerting pressure on you to change your mind. Exhibiting anger, sadness, or frustration when you do not give consent. Ignoring verbal or nonverbal cues that indicate you are not giving your consent.

Reflect and Act

Reflect: Think about a relationship in your life that matters to you. How do you ask each other for consent? How do you give each other your consent? Do these behaviors encourage and support freely given and voluntary consent? Do this for more of the different relationships in your life. Are there patterns to be found in either the requesting or giving of consent? What patterns are positive? Which could use work?

Act: We often think of consent as only being a part of intimate exchanges with relationship partners. But consent matters everywhere. So practice asking for consent in everyday situations. Practice asking consent for everyday touch ("May I give you a hug goodbye?" "May I reach over into your space to show you where the button is on your laptop?"). Practice asking consent for everyday privacy questions ("Is it okay if I share with a friend of mine that you enjoy anime too?" "Is it okay if I tell a friend your middle name? They have the same one!"). Practicing consent this way makes you more confident in having more intimate consent conversations, plus it models to the people in your life the kind of consent questions you'd appreciate being asked.

TOOL #3: BOUNDARIES

What are boundaries?

Boundaries are the limits we set for ourselves in relationships in order to keep us safe and healthy.

You can think of boundaries as a regulatory system, maintaining the integrity of things that are important to us. Boundaries help us keep our bodily and emotional autonomy intact. Boundaries support our decisions around consent. And boundaries articulate our values and beliefs as actions. If we hold some part of our life, our body, or our emotional state valuable, we can use boundaries to protect it.

Boundaries are for *us*. They are about us. They concern what we will and won't do, what we will and won't enjoy. When boundaries start to concern other things or focus on other people, we can run into trouble. Now, our boundaries certainly *respond* to the actions of others, but we have to think of our boundaries as something that surrounds us and our actions, not as something that surrounds and restricts others.

Boundaries exist in every relationship, not just the ones that are sexual or romantic. All the ways in which we are in relationship with other people require us to know, communicate, and enforce some boundaries. So while that includes romantic and sexual relationships, it also includes friendships, work relationships, hobby partners, and neighbors. "Relationship," as always, is broadly understood here, and all forms have their health maintained by boundaries.

Why do boundaries matter for aspec folks?

It takes a lot of work to understand ourselves as aspec folks, not only to learn what we want and what we don't for our bodies and our relationships, but also to *embrace* and stand confidently in what we want and what we don't. The world works hard to make us question those things, feel ashamed of those things, and discard those things in exchange for a more allonormative way of being. To be an aspec person means you're putting in hard work, and that work deserves to be protected.

Boundaries help us do that. When we set boundaries with other people, we're asking them and showing them the correct way to respect the work we've done for ourselves. We're showing them the correct way to respect our aspec experience.

What do good boundaries look like?

One way to establish fair, clear, and strong boundaries is to think of each boundary as having two parts: a cause and an effect. This structure for boundaries explains to a partner the action you are intending to take in order to take care of yourself if certain situations arise. They're "if/then" statements: *if* this action occurs or situation arises, *then* I will respond in this way.

Two really important things here.

First, the "if" part of your boundary needs to be clear. It can't be fuzzy or ill-defined. It's got to be a clear action or clear situation. "If you make me feel weird..." isn't a good foundation for a fair, clear, and strong boundary. It's too unclear. It could change day to day. It could be very inconsistent. A stronger boundary would begin, "If you say very flirty things to me after I've asked you not to..." *That's* clear, and it will help your boundary be a successful one.

Second, the "then" part of your boundary needs to be about *you*. It needs to be about your actions and your adjustments to the given situation. Because that's who you can control. As much as we'd like to decide for other people how they will behave towards us, we can't control what they will choose to do. So you'll never create a fair, clear, and strong boundary if it attempts to dictate how another person will behave. Your strength lies in what *you* decide to do, so build your boundaries on that foundation.

For example, let's say you and your romantic partner have made some agreements about what kind of touch is okay when you're close. You've decided that it's okay to kiss, it's okay to caress, and it's okay to press your bodies together. But you're not okay with them touching your genitals or nipples, and you're not okay with them touching you with their genitals, even through clothes.

But your partner has a habit of pushing past these agreements when you're close. The oversteps are usually small—they'll move a hand very close to your genitals or they'll grind against you a little while you're making out—but they're still oversteps.

A less successful boundary would be "If we're close, then you can't push the edges of our agreements anymore." That's a demand on *their* behavior. That's a limit on what they can do. You've set the boundary, but you've got no control over it. This doesn't protect the work you've done for yourself, and it leaves all the decision making to them.

Instead, a more successful boundary would be "If we're close and you push beyond what we've agreed is okay physically, then I will stop our intimacy." That's focused on your actions. It's focused on what you will do to care for yourself. They are still allowed full autonomy to make the choices they want to make—yes, they can still decide to do the thing you didn't agree to—but you have now established a clear consequence and you have control over the success of this boundary.

A good boundary is also responsive to the person and relationship it's being set for. Boundaries cannot be one-size-fits-all, because each person in our lives has different values, experiences, and capabilities. Each relationship in our lives has different dynamics, strengths, and weaknesses. So our boundaries need to respond to that. If we make boundaries that value and protect ourselves while also considering someone else's ability to meet those expectations, we're creating boundaries that are fair and that meet the people in our lives where they are.

When we shape boundaries in this way, regardless of the kind of boundary we're setting, we are giving ourselves the best chance to live our aspec lives safely and healthily.

Building the right relationship to boundaries

Now that you're equipped with a method of building strong boundaries, let's talk about building a strong relationship to those boundaries. Making them is one thing. Incorporating them into our lives and having them support and nurture our relationships is another thing entirely.

On one end of the spectrum is having a set of boundaries that are so strict, so regimented, that very little can get inside them. This is having *rigid boundaries*. Having rigid boundaries keeps other people at a distance all the time, prevents you from experiencing any kind of intimacy with the people you're in relationship with, and can isolate you from having full, bountiful relationships. We can, as aspec folks, tend towards rigid boundaries, because we've experienced so much of the world pushing very hard to try to change us. Being strict and being vigilant can feel very protective to us. But rigid boundaries can sometimes protect us out of the things we want and enjoy.

On the opposite end of the spectrum is having a set of boundaries that is loose and ill-defined. Or it's having boundaries we don't consistently enforce. This is having *porous boundaries*. Having porous boundaries presents the opposite problem. Too much gets in. Too much is allowed. While we know and understand where we want the line to be between what we want and what we don't want, porous boundaries don't keep those things on their correct sides. It can lead us to feel out of control, to feel not in our power, or to feel that we do not deserve to have what our boundaries are designed to protect. Aspec folks develop porous boundaries when we fear that asserting our wants and needs will lead to rejection. That fear is natural to experience—no one wants to feel the sting of rejection—but when that fear causes us to loosen our boundaries too much, it can lead to other negative consequences.

What we want are *healthy boundaries*, boundaries that are firm and keep harm at bay, but that are also pliable enough to allow people and feelings and experiences in. Healthy boundaries are assertive but not inflexible. They are generous but not ineffective. They meet us and the people in our lives where we are. Healthy boundaries create the space where you can engage authentically and fully in your relationships, as you are.

How do I communicate my boundaries?

Wouldn't it be great if when we figured out what our boundaries are, they would magically teleport into the brains and hearts of our relationship partners? No talking, just *knowing*, and all of our limits, needs, and wants would be respected and understood?

Maybe someday. But for now, we have to get good at communicating our boundaries.

Communicate the reason the boundary exists. A good place to start is identifying what's causing you to set a boundary and why it's causing you to set it. "I've been uncomfortable when we've been sharing intimate space, so I want to talk to you about a boundary." "I've been frustrated by our plans starting late because we aren't meeting at the agreed time, so I want to talk to you about a boundary." "I'm feeling disrespected by some agreements not being followed, so I want to talk to you about a boundary." Your limits don't exist in a vacuum, and this helps you communicate more clearly the context for the boundary you need to set.

Share your boundary. With the context set, you can share the "if/ then" statement of your boundary. Do this kindly but straightforwardly. Don't apologize for your boundaries. Setting limits for your own safety and health is not something to be sorry for. But try to avoid being too "nice." It's okay if the conversation is uncomfortable. It's okay if what you have to say feels hard. It is kinder for you to be direct, clear, and honest than it is for you to be "nice."

Stick to your boundary. Now that you've shared it, it's time to stick to it. Show your boundary the respect you want others to show it. That means following through on the consequences if the boundary isn't honored. That means not treating your boundary as though it's unreasonable or unfounded. That means not apologizing for setting or keeping your boundaries. We don't have to write people off when they cross a boundary. Being empathetic and giving second chances is fine if you're protecting your safety and health. But we show ourselves respect and we show our relationships respect when we stick to the boundaries we set.

It's time to talk about "no"

The three relationship tools of this chapter—autonomy, consent, and boundaries—all focus on understanding and defining our limits. Part of achieving that is learning to say "no."

Saying "no" is one of the most important skills we can learn, but it's a skill many people have trouble mastering. We fear the conflict and tension that comes with saying "no." We avoid saying "no" in order to avoid disappointing people or creating hurt feelings. Also, human relationships center reciprocity, or the practice of ensuring some shared benefit through mutual exchange. That back and forth is the expected way all relationships will work, so when we want to say "no," we're disrupting that reciprocity, and it can feel as though we're threatening our relationships ourselves.

But saying "no" is vital in ensuring our bodies, minds, and borders remain safe and healthy. Let's look at some ways we can strengthen our skill in saying "no" and ways we can make it more effective every time.

Practice and prepare. Practice makes perfect, and saying "no" is no exception. We can bolster our confidence in saying "no" by thinking through the ways we are comfortable saying "no." Try on different bits of language. Run through scenarios in your head. Come up with a list of different ways to say "no" that make you feel empowered. Having a plan makes it easier in the moment.

Keep things clear. A clear "no" is a strong "no." Be clear about what you're saying "no" to and, if you want and are able to share, be clear about what priorities are causing the "no." Things like "I won't be able to do that, because I have other plans" or "I don't feel comfortable doing that, because I've set some boundaries around that for myself" or "I don't think this is for me, because I'm not feeling comfortable in this situation" are all ways to be clear about your "no."

Let your "no" stand. The way another person feels about your "no" is none of your business. Once you've said "no," let your "no" stand. Reiterate it if you get pushback, but do your best to stand your ground and not deviate from it. If you're getting pushback that makes you uncomfortable, you can acknowledge their feelings ("I know you might feel it's unfair, but…") or calmly state your own ("I am feeling frustrated and disappointed that you're not accepting what I'm saying"), but don't back down.

"No" has limits

It's important here to acknowledge, again, where our intersections can complicate our relationship to these tools.

Aspec folks experiencing other forms of systemic oppression—racism, misogyny, transphobia, homophobia, ableism, and the like—will have more complex experiences with the power of "no." When power dynamics are shaped by these other dimensions of oppression, aspec folks living at those intersections may experience diminished capabilities of saying "no." So while an aspec person may feel in their power to use their "no" in relation to their aspec-ness, the weight of other oppressions they face may limit, diminish, or erase their "no."

Again, we cannot fully liberate aspec folks to live their truths unless we are simultaneously fighting against other forms of oppression.

Our "no" is valuable to us

We are told, from the moment we recognize our ace or aro identities, that we are less worthy of our "no." We are told that our aspec identity is either a brokenness, proof that something is faulty in our makeup, or is an absence, proof that we are missing something essential that everyone else has. We are told that since we come to the table with less, we are entitled to less, and that even if we want to say "no," we should defer, should forfeit our "no."

But we deserve our "no." The things you want as an aspec person, the things you choose, the things that come from the wholeness of who you are and that express that wholeness are not less than. You deserve to say "yes" to things you want, and you deeply deserve to say "no" to what you don't. Even if you want to say "no" to everything society expects of you, your "no" is entirely, irrevocably yours.

Allow your "no" to help you shape the relationships—and the life—you say "yes" to.

Boundaries red flags

Here are some words and actions that help you identify when a relationship partner isn't respecting your boundaries.

Words: "You're making a big deal out of nothing." "I don't think what I did was a problem, so you shouldn't either." "You're not really going to do anything about it." "You didn't say anything about this, so you're being unfair to me now." "I have control of [insert resource], so I think you'll let me keep doing this."

Actions: Doing the behaviors that you've set boundaries around, but becoming angry when you follow through on consequences. Gaslighting you into thinking you didn't set clear boundaries. Removing access to resources they have control over to manipulate your boundaries.

Reflect and Act

Reflect: Think about a relationship in your life where you feel your boundaries are respected. How do you articulate those boundaries to that person? How do they demonstrate their respect for your boundaries? Think about someone in your life you feel comfortable saying "no" to. Why do you feel comfortable with this person? How do they respond to your "no"? What qualities in that relationship nurture a space in which "no" is valued?

Act: While we may feel empowered to set our boundaries, following through on consequences can feel daunting and difficult. Enlist a trusted friend to help you practice enacting consequences. Choose a boundary you feel anxious about following through on, and practice the conversation with this trusted friend. Make sure you practice restating your boundary, restating why it's important, and restating the consequence. Ask your trusted friend to give you some pushback, so you can practice standing your ground. Use these practice conversations to grow courage and confidence around following through on your boundaries.

Chapter 4

What We Owe Each Other

Communication, Commitment, and Compromise

I want to talk about *Frankenstein*.

You know how in the movie Dr. Frankenstein is cloistered away in his laboratory, obsessively working toward this incredible (but probably monstrous) goal of reanimating human flesh and creating life? He's just *obsessed* with it. All his moments are focused on this mad experiment. He's bossing Igor around. He's adjusting knobs and switches. He's delivering feverish soliloquies. Everything is focused on making this creature stitched together from grave-robbed human parts a living, breathing thing?

And he does it. All this fiery obsession actually makes a monster. His single-minded ambition and dogged pursuit actually *work*. And the creature is, as Dr. Frankenstein so effusively screams in the movie, *ALIIIIIVE!*

Then the monster freaks out, escapes, kills some people, and generally throws things into chaos.

The first phase of my Big Ace Life kinda felt that way to me.

At first, I was Dr. Frankenstein, working feverishly in the lab to create my asexuality. I was figuring out how I wanted to define it, what labels I wanted to use, what I wanted in my physical relationships, where my boundaries were, what my relationship to sex was, what my relationship to other kinds of intimacy was, what I was willing to do, what I wasn't willing to do. I was stitching all the pieces of my asexuality together, stitching together this new version of myself, and my whole experience of being ace was wrapped up in that internal journey.

Then I came out. And the creature was *alive*. And just as in *Frankenstein*, my deeply considered and obsessively thought-through asexuality, though very well meaning, kind of freaked out when it interacted with the world. My existing relationships got very complicated very quickly. Other people didn't know what to do with it. I didn't know how to inhabit my ace identity with other people. What was under control in the lab was running amok in the streets.

Thankfully, things turned out better for my aceness than they did for Dr. Frankenstein's Creature. (Sorry, pal.) But there's something to be said about what happens when our asexuality has to move from our interior world into our exterior one. That translation isn't easy, and it requires a completely different set of tools.

In the last chapter, we looked at three tools that help us articulate and assume control over what happens within us. In this chapter, we're turning our vision outwards, towards the people we choose to enter in relationship with, and considering what we need to build a shared space with them, a space that honors everyone's wants, needs, and understandings of themselves.

We'll do that by looking at three more relationship tools: communication, commitment, and compromise.

TOOL #4: COMMUNICATION

It would be a fool's errand to try to condense the basics of good communication into a short chunk of this chapter. I could write an entire book about good communication, and that book would sit next to hundreds of other books about good communication already on the shelves. So we'll cover the most important basics in our communication survival kit, and we'll focus on what our relationship to communication should look like.

Communication is a two-way street

Communication is the process where you and your relationship partner share thoughts, feelings, and experiences that are important to you and work to reach mutual understanding of those thoughts, feelings, and experiences.

It's important to think of communication as an exchange, a two-way street that you and your relationship partner travel together. The sharing is mutual. The understanding is mutual. If the communication bends too far in one direction, if either side of the communication is dominating the time, taking up all the air and space, and not letting the other side be heard, it's not good communication.

This two-way street isn't built only through listening. It requires a conscious effort on the part of everyone involved to give equal weight and respect to both sides. We have to be thoughtful that the space we're making can hold and consider both sides with care.

Communication is a classroom

We can improve the quality of our communication with relationship partners if we think of communication as a classroom.

The space we create in communication with a relationship partner is a space in which we can teach and learn. We can teach our relationship partners about how we feel, how we process experiences, what our boundaries are, what our values are, and what it means to move through the world as us. And it's a space where we can learn all of those things about our relationship partner.

Approaching communication with a sense of curiosity and a spirit of learning makes communication more open, more empathetic, and more successful. When we see that space as a space to grow our understanding of the people we're in relationship with, as opposed to simply a space where we're getting our point across, we will be communicating more deeply.

This way of thinking about communication is important for aspec folks. Our identities remain largely misunderstood by most people we encounter. Even with the best of intentions, the people we choose to be in relationship with can carry stereotypes, misconceptions, and biases with them into our interactions. Communication with the spirit of the classroom becomes a space to dispel those erroneous ideas of who we are, and by doing so expand the community of those who see and respect aspec folks for who we truly are.

Communication is a workshop

Communication deepens and becomes more useful when we think of it as a workshop.

Often, we enter communication with our relationship partners with the goal of being heard. And that's a great goal. It's an essential part of communication. But if we're communicating simply to be heard, we miss one of communication's strengths: it builds something new.

Good communication—that curious, openhearted exchange that upholds and uplifts both sides of the engagement—creates something new that wasn't there before. It builds windows so we can see each other more clearly. It builds doors that open onto deeper understandings of each other. It builds bridges across disagreements. It builds new structures that protect us and the bonds we value.

Thinking about communication as a building space discourages the employment of destructive tactics—things like blame, dishonesty, name calling, shutting down—and focuses us on constructive goals. When communication is a workshop, our relationships stand on more solid ground.

Communication is self-advocacy

If there is one mental framework for communication that I believe is the most valuable, it's the idea that communication is self-advocacy.

Being aspec in a world that actively works to deny our existence makes it difficult to assert ourselves and own the space we deserve to occupy. We run into a myriad of obstacles: unkindness, misconceptions, stereotypes, ignorance, queerphobia, aphobia, lack of compassion, lack of empathy. The majority of our relationships require us to show up not only authentically as ourselves but also as our own aspec advocate, educating others about what it truly means to be aspec.

The communication of our consent, of our boundaries, of our commitments, of our feelings, of our experiences, and of our truth is helping us tell the aspec story. It tells the story of how we move through our aspec identity. It tells the larger story of how ace and aro identities move through the world. Communication is our activism, in small ways and large.

The stronger we are as communicators—both of the specifics of our own lives and of the larger truths of aspec experience—the more we combat the invisibility and misunderstanding of ace and aro folks everywhere.

The Communication Survival Toolkit

As I said earlier, it would be a fool's errand to try to offer you all the tools for good communication within this short section. But I can offer you a compact Communication Survival Toolkit which will get you started down the path to powerful, effective communication.

Be mindful of the time and place. Be thoughtful about where and when you're engaging your relationship partner in communication. Not every subject and not every conversation is right for every time and place. Sensitive subjects maybe shouldn't be discussed in a crowded café. A not-very-important discussion about the weekend maybe shouldn't happen when your relationship partner is trying to meet an urgent deadline. Finding the right time and place will ensure what you need to communicate won't get drowned out before you even start.

Use "I" statements. "I" statements focus on your feelings and your experiences instead of attempting to speak for your relationship partner's feelings and experiences. Using "I" statements keeps you from engaging in negative communication tactics like blaming, accusing, threatening, or being defensive. They allow you to communicate what you need to communicate without your relationship partner shutting down or putting them in defense mode. These statements look like "I feel..." or "I think..." or "My experience was..." Use "I" statements to sharpen and focus your communication.

Listen to understand, not to reply. It can be very easy for us, particularly in difficult conversations, to focus on formulating a response or devising a strong counterpoint. We can find ourselves listening only to shape how we will reply. This doesn't make for good communication. When we are listening, our goal should be to understand what our relationship partner is trying to say. What do they feel? What did they experience? What do they want? How did they see the situation? Remember, communication is a two-way street, and listening to understand is one way to ensure it is one.

Reflect what you hear. A great tool to make sure you're truly understanding your relationship partner is to reflect what you hear. At pivotal moments in a conversation, after giving your relationship partner all the space they need to be heard, reflect back to them what you understood. "So, what I'm hearing is..." or "What I'm understanding you to say is..." are great ways to begin reflecting. This way, your relationship partner can confirm or clarify. You're showing that you're actively listening and being fully present for them.

Try not to interrupt. Communication can get intense and engaged, and it can be easy for us to jump in when an idea that feels important hits us. But interrupting our relationship partner while they are trying to communicate is an easy way to muddle communication. Interrupting makes your relationship partner feel unheard and their ideas and experiences not valued. It also prevents you from understanding what they're trying to get across. So give them space. Don't interrupt. Stay active in your listening, and when the floor is yours, it's yours.

Choose clarity over kindness. When things get sticky in communication, we can slide into murkiness in an attempt to be kind. We can fudge the truth a little or bend our words to soften the blow. We can omit our true feelings in pursuit of "being nice." While this might feel good in the moment, in the long run this is less than effective. Choose being clear over being kind. Don't elide the truth. Don't omit your feelings. When we are direct, complete, and clear, we are showing our relationships and ourselves the most respect. We don't have to be mean to be clear. We can be gentle and respectful. But clarity should remain the priority.

Consider your nonverbal communication. Communication isn't just about our words. We can communicate a lot to a relationship partner through nonverbal communication. Be aware of what our bodies are saying while we communicate with our relationship partners. Are we projecting defensive body postures? Are we making an angry face? Are we avoiding eye contact and appearing disinterested? Are we holding our bodies in a threatening way? We can't always control what our bodies do (or how our relationship partners read that nonverbal communication), but we can be mindful of certain patterns we have in our bodies when we're engaging. Either we can actively work to create new behaviors or we can make sure our relationship partners are aware of our unique patterns and understand what they do and do not communicate. This can be an ongoing process, but it helps make your communication stronger.

Communication red flags

Here are some words and actions that can help you identify when a relationship partner isn't participating in good communication.

Words: "No, I know what you're really saying. What you're really saying is..." "What you're saying is stupid/dumb/pointless." "I don't have to listen to you, but you have to listen to me." "No, I think you're done talking now."

Actions: Interrupting you when you're trying to talk. Talking over you when you're trying to talk. Doing other things (like checking their phone) when you're trying to talk. Walking away when you're trying to talk. Yelling or raising their voice to get control of the conversation. Threatening physical violence to get control of the conversation. Using dismissive or rude nonverbal communication while you're trying to talk.

Reflect and Act

Reflect: Go through the Communication Survival Toolkit and consider your use of each skill. Which do you implement well in your communication? Which do you struggle with? Think through the list of tools in relation to your relationship partners. Which do they do well? Which do they struggle with? In each relationship, share what you've learned and make a plan with your relationship partners to work collaboratively on these skills.

Act: Use gratitude conversations to practice communication. Choose some quality, behavior, or action of someone in your life that you feel gratitude for. Share that gratitude in a conversation, and use that conversation to practice some skills. Use "I" statements to explain why you feel gratitude. Ask questions about the quality or experience you're grateful for.

Reflect something you hear them explain or share with you. Be an active listener. Not only will these positive conversations help you deepen your confidence in your communication skills, but you'll be deepening your connections with people in your life.

TOOL #5: COMMITMENT

Why is commitment important?

Commitment is the mutual agreement between you and others to work together to achieve shared goals or live shared values.

We often hear about commitment in the context of a romantic relationship—"Yes, I'm in a committed relationship with my girlfriend!" "We've finally taken the leap into a committed relationship!"—but commitment is an essential part of every kind of relationship. We make commitments to our friends. We make commitments to our coworkers. We make commitments to our communities. If we're wanting a connection to be nurtured and to last, commitment will be a part of it.

Commitment takes whatever relationship we're in and gives it shape. Commitment defines the borders of a relationship, helping determine things like relationship intensity, how the relationship can grow, or what priority the relationship takes in everyone's lives. Even the small-scale commitments, the ones that address the day-to-day functions of our relationships, help define a relationship's shape. Commitment helps us know what to expect from relationships and what the relationship can expect from us.

Commitment also helps shape the *action* of a relationship, what a particular relationship *does*. We can commit to relationships that are about security, home, and raising a family. We can commit to relationships that are just about hanging out. We can commit to relationships that focus on casual sex, or sharing a hobby, or providing emotional support without practical entanglements. What we commit to communicates where we want a relationship to go or where we are open to a relationship going.

Commitment also helps define the values a relationship will uphold. A couple that believes exclusivity is an important value will commit to monogamy. A friendship group that believes it's important to maintain regular connection will commit to one night a week having coffee together. A neighborhood that believes in mutually providing for each other may commit to weekend clean-ups in a local park. The commitments we make to and with other people in relationships articulate what matters to us both individually and collectively.

Finally, commitment helps build trust. We'll explore trust in more detail in the next chapter, so we won't discuss it much here. But the process of making commitments and fulfilling them builds trust between you and the people you're in relationship with.

Commitment is not exclusivity

When we talk about commitment in relationships, most people think that means becoming monogamous, no longer looking for dates or other romances, deprioritizing other relationships like friendships, and focusing on the primary relationship and building it towards the future. We tend to equate commitment with sexual and romantic exclusivity and with moving a relationship towards marriage.

All of these are *kinds* of commitments, but they aren't what commitment *is* in totality. These are commitments that follow the social scripts that heteronormativity, amatonormativity, mononormativity, and the Relationship Escalator set forth for all of us. But not all relationships follow these scripts. In fact, most do not, and most don't require these scripts to be successful or fulfilling.

That's why it's important for us to pull the idea of commitment apart from the idea of sexual and romantic exclusivity. *All* relationships need commitment to work, because all relationships require shared goals to work toward and shared values to get there.

This is of particular importance for aspec folks. In the limited view of what commitment entails, the relationships we often seek to build are pushed to the periphery. Platonic relationships, relationships without sex, relationships without romance, relationships without exclusivity, and relationships that blur the boundaries are not seen as something worth committing to if you think commitment is simply about sexual and romantic exclusivity.

But we know you *can* build powerful, lasting relationships without sex or romance. You can build deeply committed friendships. You can build committed life partnerships. You can build queerplatonic relationships. You can build intentional family units. Commitment can provide the foundation for many human networks that defy heteronormative, allonormative, and amatonormative expectations.

What do different kinds of commitments look like?

If commitment is bigger than just sexual and romantic exclusivity, what does commitment in the broader sense look like?

Commitment is a promise we'll do something, be something, or hold a shared value for the people we're in a relationship with. That promise has conditions—the time frame for the promise or what we need promised in return—and the expectation is that, barring any condition not being met, we'll do what was promised. This works the same way for the commitments people make to us.

So any time, in any relationship, we're creating this kind of exchange, it's commitment. Whether that's in a friendship, a dating situation, a family dynamic, or a 20-year marriage.

Let's break this broad idea down into some bite-size nuggets, to make what commitment looks like easier to digest.

"Do" commitments. We can think about "do" commitments as the commitments we make in the moment or commitments that shape our daily actions. This can look like taking care of the dishes when you say you're going to, meeting a friend for dinner at the time you agreed upon, agreeing to be the designated driver for the weekend night out. These are commitments we make that we can fulfill pretty quickly, sometimes even as soon as we make them. "Do" commitments build the foundation of our relationships. We do things to help, support, and care for the people in our lives. They do things to help, support, and care for us. "Do" commitments make up our regular interactions in our relationships, and in many ways these small-scale commitments are the fundamental components of the relationships we build.

"Be" commitments. We can think about "be" commitments as the commitments we make about who we'd like or are able to be for our relationship partners. These stretch over a longer period of time and require a deeper level of investment. Unlike "do" commitments, we fulfill the promise of "be" commitments over and over, in a multitude of ways, until we mutually agree to change them. This can look like committing to be someone's boyfriend or girlfriend. This can look like agreeing on your relationship being monogamous or open. This can look like agreeing to the terms of your employment contract. It can look like establishing your relationship with someone as strictly platonic. "Be" commitments explain who you are in relation to other people—who you are to them, who they are to you—and they draw boundaries around what kind of "do" commitments one might expect. It's not a perfect science. Every relationship is its own thing. But "be" commitments shape the longer paths in our relationships.

"Us" commitments. We can think about "us" commitments as the Big Picture commitments relationship partners make together. "Us" commitments decide how individual lives become entangled (committing to moving in together, committing to sharing finances, committing to providing care for each other when things get tough), or they can define the values to be shared among the people within a relationship or community (committing to the values of the organization you work for, committing to helping neighbors keep the community clean and safe, committing to always making sure no friend drives home drunk). "Us" commitments help shape the other kinds by ensuring that everyone involved understands what the relationship is intended to be.

Taken together, these three kinds of commitments form the shape and scope of our relationships, as they relate to what we want and what we consent to.

Making commitments

Making strong, clear commitments in our relationships not only helps our partners but helps us protect ourselves. The clearer we are about what we can do, what we can be, and what we are together in our relationships, the less likely we'll be expected to do and be things we aren't comfortable with. Clear commitments can be a powerful tool for aspec folks in creating aspec-affirming space.

Be clear with yourself about what you can and can't commit to. If there's one thing that's essential in making commitments in relationships, it's being honest and clear with yourself about what's possible. It's natural to want to avoid disappointing the people we care about. But making commitments we know we can't stick to is postponing the inevitable. Sure, sometimes we will think we can do something, but we can't. Sometimes external conditions make holding a commitment impossible. But the greatest respect we can pay ourselves and our relationship partners is to be clear about what we can and can't do, and make commitments accordingly.

Make sure your commitments line up with your boundaries. Our boundaries provide a useful guide when making commitments. If well designed, our boundaries paint a picture of what we can do or be within our held values. As we make commitments, measuring them against our boundaries—and making sure they're within them—keeps us acting in our own best interest. Does what I'm committing to breach my boundaries? If yes, we need to rethink our commitment. If no, following through will uphold our values.

Stay flexible in the face of change. It's important we think of our commitments in the same way we think of ourselves: as living, evolving creatures capable of change. This is true of us as individuals. It is true of our relationships. We will grow. Our relationships will grow. And what we are capable of and open to within our relationships will change. So our commitments need to possess flexibility. Be open about changes in what you're willing and able to commit to. Sure, the bigger commitments will require harder conversations and lengthier processes of change, but it's safer and healthier to have your commitments reflect your real capabilities.

Commitments, giving in, and the fear of missing out

As we've discussed before, our normative Big Baddies set up expectations for all of us around different kinds of relationships. Friendships will look like *this*. Dating will look like *this*. Romantic relationships will look like *that*. And because those expectations are so powerful and prevalent, there are assumptions about the kinds of commitments each type of relationship will contain.

For most people, these assumptions work out. They're willing to commit to the normative expectations of different kinds of relationships, because those expectations line up with their capabilities and orientations. But for aspec folks, these assumptions don't work. We may want different things out of our relationships. We may be capable of giving different things. There are expectations we are not going to be able to meet. So we are often arriving at our relationships with a desired set of commitments that create friction with the ones that are assumed.

It's easy for us to think, "I'm the problem. *I'm* asking for more than I'm supposed to. So I should just give in and go with what's expected; otherwise, I'll miss out on having anything at all."

What we want is not the problem. The pressure to commit to things we don't want to or cannot do is a pressure to move us away from ourselves, and that is a pressure that should be avoided as much as we are able. If saying "This is what I am able to do, this is who I am able to be, and this is what I want us to be together" is not enough for someone, *you are not missing out on something*. You've avoided a relationship that didn't meet your needs, and you've stood up for who you are and what you want.

We will be our best aspec selves when our commitments are true to what we want and can do. Our relationships are honored when our commitments come from our wholly authentic selves. Don't let the fear of missing out push you to accept relationships that do not nurture and care for your aspec identity.

What if I don't fulfill my commitment to someone I'm in a relationship with?

It's inevitable that we will sometimes fall short of our commitments. At every level—from the smallest "do" commitment to the largest "us" commitment—obstacles can arise that prevent us from following through on things we commit to, even with the best of intentions. Layer on the complexities of moving through aspec experience, where societal pressures and our own evolving understandings of our bodies and minds can change what we're capable of and willing to do, and there are many opportunities for our commitments to outpace us.

When we don't fulfill the commitments we make to relationship partners, it's important we do a few key things:

Acknowledge where we fell short of our commitment. Be present. Be clear. Be truthful. Owning that you didn't meet a commitment is a foundation for repairing any damage. "I recognize I didn't pick you up at the time we agreed on." "I recognize I said we'd communicate daily by text, and I haven't succeeded at that." "I recognize I said I wanted our relationship to become more serious, and I'm not showing up in the ways you expected." This is not about justifying yourself. This is not about giving context. This is about acknowledging that a commitment was made, but a different outcome transpired. Acknowledging this in you also acknowledges the experience of your relationship partner, and it puts you on the same page.

Provide context, but don't make excuses. It's important to share, where you're able, the reasons and context for why you didn't fulfill the commitment. "I got distracted, and didn't watch the time." "I was surprised with some unexpected work, and I forgot to do what was asked." "I thought I would be able to text you daily, but I'm realizing in practice it's not a style I'm good at maintaining." "I believed I would be comfortable with a more serious relationship when we discussed it, but my feelings have changed, and I understand my wants and needs differently now." Use this time to help your relationship partner understand why the commitment wasn't fulfilled. You're giving context for clarity, not for absolution. The information you share here is for the benefit of your relationship partner, not for you. Some of this may be uncomfortable, depending on the size of the breach and the scope of the commitment, but focus on being as clear as you can.

Present a way forward. Offer your ideas for how to move beyond this moment. That may look like an apology and a recommitment to getting the task done. It may look like giving space for your relationship partner to express how they feel and a shared agreement to work harder in the future. It may look like presenting a new commitment with new parameters that better match your capabilities. Or it may look like a renegotiation of the boundaries and substance of the relationship in question. Some of these adjustments are easy. Others are painfully hard. But in all cases, offering some path to take together in pursuit of commitments that are better suited to you both is the best action to take.

Listen and respect your relationship partner's space. Throughout all of this, keep your ears and your heart open to your relationship partner. If they have tough feelings, make space for that. If it takes them a while to decide what path forward they'd like to take, allow that time. If they have ideas of their own, be open and collaborate on a solution together. Our actions don't exist in a vacuum. What we do and sometimes what we don't do impacts our relationship partners. Hold space for that.

What if someone doesn't fulfill their commitment to me?

In an ideal world, our relationship partners will provide us with all of the respect and sensitivity described above. Sometimes we'll get that. Sometimes we won't. But in every case, there are a few things to remember when someone doesn't fulfill a commitment made to us.

We are allowed our feelings. It hurts sometimes when a commitment is broken. Sometimes we can get angry. Sometimes it triggers insecurities and self-doubt. None of those feelings are fun for us, but we are allowed them and they should be respected. Don't let anyone tell you that you shouldn't feel what you feel, even if there's a good reason the commitment was broken. You don't process difficult feelings by pushing them down and brushing them away. They don't have to run the show, but acknowledging them and giving them space makes getting to the other side of them easier.

Don't accept blame. Unless you intentionally worked to thwart your relationship partner from fulfilling a commitment—and why would you do that? That's not healthy behavior—you are not to blame for a commitment being broken. Aspec folks encounter this issue often. Our identities are often blamed for our relationship partners not meeting their commitments. And because we are conditioned to believe our identities are a brokenness, we believe that broken relationships are our fault by default. But we don't control the actions of others. Who we are is not to blame for how someone else chooses to behave. Do not accept blame for what you are not responsible for.

If useful, create a boundary. One way we can move forward is to articulate a boundary around the issues at play. "If the commitment to pick me up at 3:30 doesn't get kept again, then we'll just drive separately in the future." "If staying in communication through text daily continues to be inconsistent, then I'll ask for different ways to feel connected to you." "If this relationship continues to move in a direction that doesn't align with my needs and wants, then I'll reconsider whether this relationship is one I want to continue being a part of." A boundary establishes a way forward, and it keeps you protected and within your values and needs.

Do what you can. Do what you want. Do what is you

Our commitments are expressions of who we are, so make sure your commitments are reflections of who you know yourself to be. Let your commitments show how you are aspec. Let them show what you want as an aspec person. Let them be your aspec identity in action.

Don't let others force you into commitments that aren't true to you. Don't let them blame their failed commitments on who you are. Don't hide yourself and your wants in order to make others happy.

Do what you are able to do. Do what you want to do. Do what is true and authentic to who you are.

Commitment red flags

Here are some words and actions that may help you identify when a relationship partner isn't respecting commitments.

Words: "I know I said I'd do that, but it's not a big deal." "I guess it's your fault for believing me when I said I'd do that." "I knew you'd be mad I didn't follow through, but I knew you'd let it slide."

Actions: Repeatedly making commitments and not honoring them. Reacting with anger when you point out a missed commitment. Blaming you for not honoring their commitments.

Reflect and Act

Reflect: Identify someone in your life who is very good at honoring their commitments. How do they articulate their commitments to others? How do they demonstrate living up to those commitments? What are they like when they don't fulfill a commitment? What can you learn from their behavior that you can use in your life and relationships?

Act: Make a community commitment. Connect with your local LGBTQ center or organization that works on an issue you care about. Schedule a time to volunteer and follow through on that commitment. While we can focus on interpersonal commitments, we can learn a lot about ourselves and our ability to make and make good on commitments by making them to our community. Plus, we help improve our corner of the world.

TOOL #6: COMPROMISE

What does good compromise in a relationship look like?

Compromise is a process of reaching agreement with your partner through mutual give-and-take. It's a way to honor our uniquenesses and differences while making room for those of our partner.

It can be very easy for compromise to go awry, so a good place to begin is describing what good compromise looks like. This isn't comprehensive, but it will provide you a starting place to develop healthy compromises in your relationships.

Compromise must happen in good faith. "In good faith" means that both sides of a compromise are coming to the table with good and honest intentions. Both sides are approaching compromise with a desire to reach a resolution that feels fair and truthful. One side is not trying to manipulate the other. One side is not trying to hide something from the other. Because compromise requires vulnerability and necessitates us giving some things up, we want to feel safe in the knowledge that we are doing those hard things in a space that is not trying to harm us.

Compromise requires mutual sacrifice. "Sacrifice" may feel like a strong word, but it gets the point across. In healthy compromise, both sides are giving something up to move toward the center. This does not mean you always meet exactly in the center. Sometimes we meet a little closer to the other person. Sometimes we meet a little closer to us. But both sides of a compromise should be willing to give up something to facilitate that motion toward agreement.

Compromise should have a shared goal. Just as the sacrifice of a compromise needs to be mutual, the goal of the compromise should be shared as well. It's important that both sides agree on what the outcome of the compromise might be. When the goal centers only one side of the compromise, sacrifice will move in that direction only. When the goal is shared, the sacrifice must move in both directions. Make sure your goals include words like "us," "our," and "we." Make sure the goal of compromise is constructive for both sides.

Compromise leaves room for "no." Sometimes sacrifice just isn't possible. While we want compromise to earn both sides what they want, our boundaries, our values, our needs, our consent, our autonomy, and our commitments should be honored and remain intact. Sometimes that means one side needs to say "no." Good, healthy compromise leaves space for that "no." It recognizes that sometimes the compromise is acknowledging there is no compromise possible. It commits to other solutions without attempting to be retributive.

Why do we have to compromise in relationships?

Remember how we talked about communication being a workshop, a space where things can be built between relationship partners? Compromise serves a similar function: it is a place where things that make a relationship work are built.

Relationships are always trying to master the complicated alchemy of merging different partners' needs and wants. The ideal is to honor those individual sets of needs and wants but create a third thing from their merging—the shared needs, wants, and experiences of the relationship. Compromise helps build that third thing.

When one person's needs and wants dominate a relationship—be it one friend's choices of where to eat dinner and what movie to see, or one married partner's dominance of how to spend money and when to be intimate—that relationship fails to support everyone in it. When a relationship moves in only one partner's direction, that relationship takes more than it gives.

Compromise helps relationships move closer to fairness. Yes, we give things up when we compromise, but we do so in the spirit of building something that enriches us and our relationship partners.

Can compromise be unhealthy?

It's important to be clear here: not all compromise is created equal.

While sacrifice that moves us closer to the center is an important part of making compromise work, it's important to hold that not all sacrifice is in our best interests. Not all movement toward the center is movement forward. Sometimes, the compromises we make, though in spirit a move toward an equilibrium with our relationship partner, are moves away from some essential truths of who we are.

Compromise should not move us away from our boundaries. It shouldn't move us away from what we consent to. It shouldn't move us away from making autonomous choices. Our values, our core beliefs, and our identities should not be diminished when we compromise.

Compromise should feel like an addition, not a subtraction. The shared agreement we make should honor our boundaries, honor our autonomy, and honor our consent. Meeting in the middle should celebrate our values and beliefs. We should feel as though the new things made by a compromise make who we are in ourselves and in our relationships clearer. We should feel as though it moves us and our relationship forward.

It is also important to acknowledge here that compromise is heavily impacted by the power dynamics present in a relationship, and those dynamics can create unhealthy compromise. Who we are to each other matters. If we hold some position of power (such as being an employer or a group leader), hold more power over resources (like being in control of shared money or being the only one with a car for transportation), or hold an identity that has more cultural power (such as being white or cisgender or not disabled), that power can force our relationship partners who hold identities that hold less power to make compromises that are unhealthy for them. We must be mindful of how who we are influences the way we exert power over our relationship partners, and we must be mindful of what powers our relationship partners hold that may push us into making compromises that are unhealthy for us.

How do I call out an unhealthy compromise with a relationship partner?

Recognizing unhealthy compromise is one thing. Calling it out and addressing it is another.

Here are some tips for effectively and healthily calling out unhealthy compromise in your relationships.

Don't attack. When we're on the bad end of an unhealthy compromise, anger is a natural thing to feel, and anger can push us to go on the attack with a relationship partner. But name calling, accusing, yelling, or berating are never useful tools to fix an unhealthy compromise. Remember that good communication starts with an "I" statement. Acknowledge the unhealthy compromise by talking about its impact on you. "I am feeling hurt and undervalued by the compromise we made" is a way to call your relationship partner in, so you can collaborate on fixing the problem.

Talk about the compromise, not the people. Keep your conversation focused on the compromise, and avoid making it about the people involved. "The compromise we made prevents me from spending time on my own" will feel less confrontational than "You are making me feel like I can't spend any time on my own." This keeps your communication from feeling like "you versus them," and it makes it more collaborative around a shared goal.

Offer a healthier solution. Use this moment to advocate for your needs and wants. Offer a different compromise that finds a better middle. Adjust the compromise to reflect a better acknowledgment of power dynamics. Don't be afraid to ask for what you want and need.

Be open to further compromise. Don't assume that the solutions you offer will be or should be accepted wholesale. Further compromise might be needed to meet your relationship partner in a new middle. Be open to it, and use this new round of compromise to find better ways to honor both sides and their needs.

Compromise does not mean we give up who we are

The normative social forces we talked about early in this book create a very specific expectation for aspec folks when it comes to relationships. "If you want whatever relationship you're after," these forces say, "you're going to have to be less who you are and more like us."

Aspec folks are told that whenever we want a relationship, whether it's a friendship or a date or something more like a marriage, for that relationship to work we have to move away from our aspec identity and toward an allo expectation. If we're going to have a friendship, we'll have to expect it to be diminished when our friend finds a romantic partner. If we're going to date, we'll have to include romance or sex. If we want something permanent, it's going to have to look like conventional marriage with all of its responsibilities and obligations. All of the movement is away from us, away from what we want, away from what we are.

There are many reasons we should compromise in relationships, but this is not one of them. As we work with our relationship partners to meet in the middle, we need to remember that although society believes we should give ourselves up in service of what is "normal," we deserve what we want as aspec people. Compromising our aspec identities is not something we must do in order to have relationships of all kinds. If someone asks you to give up the very things that make you aspec, that person is not working toward a healthy relationship with you.

Your aspec identity is never up for compromise.

Compromise red flags

Here are some words and actions that can help you identify when a relationship partner isn't respecting healthy compromise.

Words: "I don't think I have to give anything up." "I want you to change for what I want." "You've got to change if you want this to work."

Actions: Agreeing to compromises but not changing behaviors. Reacting in anger any time they're asked to compromise. Placing all responsibility for change on you. Refusing to compromise at all. Threatening to remove emotional or practical resources unless you make changes.

Reflect and Act

Create a compromise vision board. Somewhere that's meaningful to you or that you'll be able to refer to often, create two spaces for words and images. Label one space "Compromise I Want." Label the other "Compromise I Don't Want." In these spaces—a notebook, a Google doc, a canvas, a corkboard above your desk—put words and images that fit each category. What looks and feels like the compromise you want? What looks and feels like the compromise you don't?

Chapter 5

Centering Our Softness

Trust, Respect, Recognition, and Care

"I love you, but you know how you are. You've got hard edges."

I was in my mid-20s when my best friend said this to me over dinner. I'd been on yet another lousy date with another person who didn't "get me." No one seemed to "get me," and if they did seem to "get me," it meant they got as far away from me as they could. My romantic relationship life had been a string of dates that didn't work, boyfriends that didn't fit, and rejections I didn't fully understand.

"What is wrong with every guy in this town?" I said. "Why is it impossible for me to find someone who isn't a dead end?"

"I love you, but you know how you are," my best friend said. "You've got hard edges."

I'm sure this had been said many times to other people *about* me, but this was the first time I remember someone close to me saying this *to* me. Hard edges? What? *Me?* This particular sword was double-edged. I certainly didn't see myself as someone who had "hard edges." Hard edges *where?* And I doubly didn't appreciate her suggestion that I should already know this about myself. "You know how you are." Should I know because *you* already know? Should I know because *everyone* knows?

I don't give good poker face, so I'm sure I was staring at her with a look of confused disgust. She took a breath and plowed ahead with some tough love I needed.

"I love you, my friend, but you're *hard*. You're a hard person to me sometimes. To other people, you're a hard person *a lot* of the time. And I don't think you mean to be, but you're all walls and suspicion and judgment and things with sharp edges. And I get why you're like that. I know things have been hard for you. *People* have been hard for you. But you're taking that hardness and throwing it back at everyone instead of trying to be the thing you need from other people."

My best friend was right. (She's *always* right. Her tough love remains one of the greatest gifts of my life almost 25 years later.) It's hard to grow something nurturing and meaningful in a garden that's filled with rocks and broken glass bottles. *I* was that stony garden. And if I was going to grow the relationships I wanted, I was going to have to practice some vulnerability.

In the last two chapters, we've talked about relationship tools with harder edges: understanding our boundaries, establishing our "no," granting or rescinding consent, structuring the way we talk to each other, organizing the way we meet in the middle. These skills are drawn with clear, bold lines. In this chapter, we deal with a more porous set of skills—skills that create the space for our vulnerabilities.

Think of all the relationship tools we've learned up until now as a diving board. Think of these four relationship tools—trust, respect, recognition, and care—as the uncertain, courageous leap we make from that diving board into the waters of our relationships.

Let's talk about softness

Queer people are often defined by our hardness. We are asked to talk about how difficult accepting our queerness is for us. We are asked to recount the ways people have hurt us because of our queerness. We are painted as "fighters" and "warriors" and "survivors." We are poked and prodded into showing our anger, and then that anger is held up as indicative of who we are. We are conditioned to see our hardness as a primary tool of our queerness. We are expected to appear tough, resilient, a survivor of pain, in order to be acknowledged and taken seriously.

But our softness is as powerful a force as our hardness. In "An Essay on the Assertion of Softness as a Boundless Form of Resistance," Be Oakley talks about the ways in which our vulnerability can be a source of our strength. Oakley calls it "radical softness" and makes the point that our gentleness, our authenticity, our quiet actions, our vulnerable sharing, our queer joy are a constantly replenishable well of resistance against the forces in the world aiming to marginalize us.

We can't get through the world without our hardness. That's queer armor we need to stay alive. But we also need to celebrate our softness—lean into our softness as an armor itself—to build the deep kinds of relationships we deserve.

TOOL #7: TRUST

Trust is predicting what happens to our softness

Trust is believing we can rely on another person because they make us safe. We feel confident they will not hurt or violate us.

So much in relationships relies on softness. No matter what kind of relationship we're in, no matter what they contain, no matter their intensity, we take some piece of ourselves and hand it to another person to care for. Sometimes it's emotional softness. Sometimes it's physical softness. Sometimes we're just vulnerably sharing our skills, time, or resources with someone. But there's always the leap of faith that our softness won't hurt us.

That's trust.

Trust may be a leap, but it's not a haphazard leap into the darkness. Trust is a *calculated* leap, a prediction based on what we know, what we've been shown, and what's been committed to us. Trust also works in reverse: our relationship partners make their predictions of us based on what they know, what we've shown them, and what we've committed to them.

Trust is predicting what will happen if we are vulnerable, what will happen if we show our softness, what will happen if we hand our gentlest parts to our relationship partner. When we have generous trust in our relationship partner, our prediction is that our softness will be safe. When we have little trust in our partner, our prediction spells disaster for our softness.

The three Cs of building trust

So how can we develop generous trust? How can we ensure that our predictions of our partner will include our softness being cared for, and how can we ensure our partners predict we will care for their softness?

Show you are capable. This one's simple: do what you say. When you commit to something, follow through. When you state a belief or value, act and live accordingly. Demonstrate that you can stick to the commitments you make to *yourself*, even the small ones, even the insignificant ones. When you show a relationship partner that you are capable of meeting your commitments and walking your own talk, you build trust.

Show you are consistent. A reliable way to build generous trust is to show you are consistent. Don't show you're capable once and expect that to be the foundation of generous trust. You've got to make that capability a *pattern*. Generous trust can grow when the outcomes aren't erratic. If a person is capable of fulfilling their commitment this time, next time, the next time, and again the next time, it's easier to trust that they'll fulfill it *any* time.

Show you are courageous. There are two kinds of courageousness worth investing in. First, it takes courage to show up in any relationship and do the hard work of building trust. It's a process that isn't always easy. We arrive at relationships with very specific histories that can complicate how we understand and respond to our relationship partners. This can often flex our empathy and compassion muscles. But if we courageously show up and do that challenging work, we can foster powerful and healthy relationships. The other kind of courage is the courage to admit our shortcomings and missteps. If we fail at being capable or consistent, we should have the courage to own those failings. If we recognize there is room to improve the ways we show up for our relationship partner, we should own it as an opportunity for growth instead of a shame to hide. Both forms of courage help build generous trust with any person we are in relationship with.

What do I do when I break my relationship partner's trust?

Breaking our relationship partner's trust can feel terrible. It can make them feel terrible, too. It's one of the situations in relationships that calls for everyone's courage and commitment.

Here are some ways we can address the space in which we have broken our relationship partner's trust.

Own the fact that trust was broken. We don't do ourselves any favors when we reject responsibility for the ways in which we break trust with a relationship partner. Lying, hiding things, being intentionally evasive, gaslighting—these are all ways to dodge our role in breaking someone's trust. This behavior just deepens the wounds. As painful as it can be, as difficult as it can be, owning our responsibility for breaking trust goes a long way towards mending that trust. When we say "I know our trust is harmed, and I know the role I played in that," we are caring for our relationship partner in an important way.

Give space and grace to their hurt feelings. When a person you care for violates your trust, it sucks. You can feel betrayed. You can question whether other things you believe are true. You can feel foolish and embarrassed that you put your trust in a person. These emotions are heavy and hard. It can be easy when you're the cause of these heavy and hard feelings to minimize them, push them aside, or center the difficult feelings their hurt brings up in you as a diversion. Resist that urge. Give your relationship partner the space and grace they need to be hurt. (Your courage comes in handy here.) Let them express their pain. Validate their pain. Sit with it as they sit with it. If we cause hurt and fail to acknowledge or respect that hurt, trust is much harder to rebuild.

Behave as though you've got it until you get it. Rebuilding trust takes time. The hurt feelings and anxieties won't disappear overnight. So give your relationship partner the safest place possible to do that rebuilding. Behave as though you have their trust, even if you don't. Keep in mind that consistency is a key building block for trust, so show up consistently, and walk the road back to trust with your partner.

What do I do when my relationship partner breaks my trust in them?

Having a relationship partner betray our trust is a painful, confusing experience. It not only gives birth to difficult feelings of hurt, embarrassment, and anger, but it also can make us look at other parts of our shared experience with suspicion and anxiety. Was I right to trust them in this other context? Can I trust them in this other part of our shared experience? It's a very challenging space to move through.

When you're on the receiving end of broken trust, here are a few things you can do to navigate that space while preserving your health and safety.

Honor your feelings, but be mindful of their power. It's never fun, but you've got to feel your feelings. Feel the anger. Feel the hurt. Feel the embarrassment. If you don't allow space to feel them, those difficult feelings can twist and fester and grow into deeper wounds that may be impossible to heal. But we have to be mindful in the processing of those feelings to not let them dictate how we show up to our relationship partner. If our hurt feelings cause us to say insulting things, act in intentionally harmful ways to our relationship partner, or act in retaliation to them, we're not really doing ourselves any healing favors. Someone can hurt us, and we can feel difficult things. But we should not let that betray our own standards for ourselves.

Reinforce and adapt your boundaries. As you work through the process of building trust, take intentional time to reinforce your boundaries with your relationship partner. Make them clear. And when it fits the circumstances, adapt them to reflect how you're feeling in the moment. If the spot of broken trust causes you to have new boundaries around certain things, articulate that to your relationship partner. Reset the playing field for what's in bounds, what you expect, and what your actions will be if boundaries aren't respected. This is as much for you as it is for your relationship partner.

Not every broken trust can be rebuilt. Am I saying you have to forgive and rebuild with a relationship partner any and every time they break your trust? Absolutely not. Sometimes the broken trust is so painful and so severe that rebuilding is impossible. Sometimes an ongoing pattern of small breaks of trust adds up to a need to step away. And sometimes a breach of trust crosses a clear boundary, and we decide that's not repairable. You are always in control of who gets your trust. You don't owe any relationship partner the labor to rebuild broken trust. If you decide trust cannot be rebuilt, stand confident in that decision.

Trust red flags

Here are some words, feelings, and actions that can help you identify when you don't feel strong trust in a relationship partner.

Words: "They said they were doing this, but I think they're really doing this other thing." "I can't share this with them. I'm afraid of how they'll react." "I can't rely on them to support me in this."

Feelings: Not believing your relationship partner. Being afraid your relationship partner will judge thoughts or feelings you have.

Actions: Intentionally turning to other people for support your relationship partner has committed to give. Hiding feelings or thoughts from a relationship partner out of fear of rejection or ridicule.

Reflect and Act

Reflect: Think about someone in your life you trust deeply. What are the qualities they possess that make you trust them? What behaviors do they exhibit that make you trust them? What do you observe about the way they treat others that makes you trust them?

Act: Do a trust workout. Invite a trusted friend to a conversation. Share something personal about yourself that your friend doesn't know. It can be something small: an embarrassing story from when you were a kid, a silly picture of an old Halloween costume, a guilty pleasure you haven't told anyone about. Trust them to hold this small truth about you. Pay attention to what it feels like to overcome any anxieties you feel, and pay attention to the positive feelings that arrive when they embrace what you tell them. Working out your "trust muscles" in these small ways will help you have harder conversations about bigger truths in other situations.

TOOLS 8 AND 9: RESPECT AND RECOGNITION

We're going to take the next two tools—respect and recognition—together, because I think it's useful to consider them very close teammates in the Relationship Toolbox.

Respect is when we hold someone else's feelings, wishes, beliefs, and experiences as valid and *theirs*, and we do not interfere with or devalue those feelings, wishes, beliefs, and experiences. Recognition is the feeling of being seen, fully, for who you are by another person. It is the feeling that a person we are in a relationship with understands the basic parts that make us up, and sees those things without judgment.

Both respect and recognition are about affirmation. They ensure that partners within a relationship feel that who they are, what they are, what they value, and what they aim to become are allowed space to be and grow. If you feel respected, and you feel as though your relationship partner deeply recognizes you, you will feel safe to shine in your truest light and follow whatever path that light illuminates into your future. We do such deep and involved work for *ourselves* with the other relationship tools, and hopefully we encourage our relationship partners to do the same work for themselves. Respect and recognition show up on the scene to applaud that work, to celebrate that work, and to actively nurture what that work can make possible.

How does respect create affirming space in our relationships?

Respect has two main components: *validating* the parts that make up a person and *not interfering* with that person living and embodying those parts. When our relationship partners do both things, we feel respected. (The same holds true for us making our relationship partners feel respected, too.)

We want our relationship partners to acknowledge our aspec identity. We want them to treat it as a real thing. We want them to believe us when we talk about what that experience entails. We want them to use the language we use to talk about ourselves. We want them to believe our struggles with our aspec identity. We want them to share in the joy of our aspec identity. All of these things *validate* us as aspec people.

We want them to not make jokes at the expense of our aspec identities. We want them to see our boundaries as legitimate and understandable. We want them to honor our consent. We want them to not question our bodily and emotional autonomy. We want them to not blame our aspec identity for issues in our relationship. We want them to honor their commitments. This is what *not interfering* with living out our aspec identity looks like.

Respect doesn't mean having to understand everything about a person. Respect doesn't even mean having to *like* everything about a person. We're in relationships all the time where parts of another person are mysterious, confusing, or downright annoying. We're also in relationships where we are just as mysterious, confusing, or annoying. But we don't have to attack those parts. We don't have to demean those parts. We don't have to use them as weapons of harm against each other. We can allow them to be, and we can say, "I see that part of you, and it's cool. I may not get it, but I see it. And we're good."

That's respect, and that's affirming.

Do we have to respect everything about our relationship partners, and do they have to respect everything about us?

No, we/they do not.

When some part of another person actively crosses our boundaries, violates our consent, denies our autonomy, breaches our trust, or otherwise invalidates key parts of who we are, we do not owe that person respect for that part of them.

We also don't have to respect parts of other people that harm or invalidate other communities we are not a part of. Let's say a relationship partner is affirming of our aspec identity but is vocally and actively transphobic. Their transphobia may not impact us directly, but if it goes against some of our core values as a human being, we don't have to respect that part of them.

Everyone decides for themselves just how many of these points of friction can exist in their relationships before a relationship needs to end. Some people have higher tolerances than others, and that's okay. Make the choices that best align with both your values and your boundaries. But don't feel obligated to accept, affirm, and respect any part of someone that dehumanizes you or people around you.

How does recognition create affirming space in our relationships?

Recognition can sometimes feel a lot like respect—it's why they're packaged together like this—but it takes an extra step that respect does not. Recognition not only validates who we are and what we value, but it sees those things as immutable parts of us, things in us that play necessary roles in who we are. Recognition says, "You are these things, and these things are you."

Recognition is powerful. When we are in relationships that truly "see" us—and that is language often used when people talk about recognition—we can feel freed from so many self-destructive behaviors and thoughts. When we feel seen, we feel less shame. When we feel seen, we don't hide our interests or opinions. When we feel seen, we don't pretend to be things other than what we are. When we feel seen, we live in the totality of ourselves. It's entirely liberating. And affirming.

Recognition is transformative for aspec folks. We have often spent our lives not feeling seen. We don't feel seen by our families, our friends, our coworkers, folks we date. We don't feel seen by the world, because so much of it is designed to exclude us or render our lives invisible. Many of us don't even feel seen by ourselves, subjecting ourselves to constant questioning, doubting, self-shaming, and more. To be in relationships where we feel deeply seen rewrites the narrative we've lived as aspec folks, and it helps us write new stories that center us, uplift us, and make us feel whole.

What role can we play in developing respect and recognition in our relationships?

While respect and recognition are things we experience when other people make that space for us, there are some things we can do to develop respect and recognition in our relationships.

Walk the walk. Talk the talk. The first strategy is the most obvious. If we want to experience respect and recognition from our relationship partners, we should give respect and recognition to them. On the one hand, this is just good Relationship 101. Relationships are mutual exchanges, so we do our part by putting in what we'd like getting out. But this is also a good way to model to a relationship partner how to provide respect and recognition in a way that works for us. A beautiful byproduct of giving respect and recognition is that it cultivates a space for a person to mirror respect and recognition in return.

Use your intersections. Remember intersectionality from Chapter 1? Intersectionality advances an important idea: we are living a set of independent experiences that are dependently interacting all the time. We are never living one identity at a time, and never being seen as only one identity at a time. Instead, our identities are all showing up together, whether or not we see it. We can lift two important ideas from this to help us cultivate respect and recognition in our lives. First, our aspec identities don't exist in a vacuum. We often talk about our aspec identities as something we carry in a discrete box, separate from us, that functions independently of the rest of us. In reality, it is knit into all the parts of who we are—it's part of the fabric. And second, how other parts of us intersect with our aspec identities can be windows for others to look into our lives more deeply. The allo folks in our lives can't know what it's like to be ace or aro. There is never a window from their experience into ours if we're only looking at that singular part of us. But they can know what it's like to live at some of our other intersections. Maybe we share the same intersection of gender. Maybe race. Maybe neurodivergence. Those intersections, which cross their experience as well, can become the window for them to look into our lives and learn something of how our aspec-ness makes us who we are.

Seeing all of a part of you isn't seeing all of you

Recognition hinges on being seen in our totality, and that is a tall order. While this book celebrates our aspec identity, everything else we are is showing up to the party, too, and those identities impact how our aspec identity is experienced. We're never only aspec today, then our gender tomorrow, then our race on Thursday, then our neurotype on Saturday.

We're everything everywhere all at once.

A person who sees the totality of one part of you still isn't seeing *all* of you. Our relationship partners can't love and validate our ace or aro identities while harboring harmful ideas about some other part of us. Our identities are interlocked. They shape each other. To truly see any one part of us, you have to see everything we are.

To really see, for example, a Black woman's asexuality, you can't just see her aceness. You have to acknowledge and understand the way her Blackness and her gender experience shape that experience of aceness. To fully see an autistic trans person's experience of being aroace, you have to hold space for and understand the way their autism and their gender experience influence and define their aroace identity. The world already makes living these interlocking identities difficult. Structural oppressions accumulate at our various intersections. When we're aware and intentional about holding space for someone's intersections, we're choosing to show up on their side and not the side of a world designed to minimize or erase them.

You don't have to accept being seen for only one part of who you are. Our relationship partners don't fully see us if they only see parts and not the whole. And when we show up for our relationship partners, we need to hold space for all the parts of their experience.

You can't be seen if you're hiding

It's hard to give you concrete tips on how to experience recognition with a relationship partner. There's no easy route to it. But an easy route to *not* being seen fully by your relationship partner is hiding yourself from them.

Maybe we're afraid of outright rejection. Maybe we're afraid the relationship will change if we show them our true self. Maybe we're hiding parts of ourselves because we're uncomfortable with them. Maybe we're hiding parts of us we hate. Whatever our reason for diminishing, pretending, or hiding, we're denying ourselves an opportunity to experience recognition.

The pressure to twist ourselves into a more socially and culturally palatable version of ourselves so that people build relationships with us is a formidable pressure. And when we give in to that pressure, we can feel rewarded. People like us! They think we're worthy! They want to be in a relationship with us! It can *feel* like recognition.

But it's not *our* recognition. It's some made-up person's recognition. And you deserve more than someone else's recognition. So, within the boundaries of you remaining safe and healthy, show up in your relationships as your full self.

Respect and Recognition red flags

Here are some feelings and actions that might indicate you aren't experiencing respect or recognition from your relationship partner.

Feelings: Feeling ashamed of parts of yourself. Feeling embarrassed of truths about you. Feeling afraid to reveal truths about you. Feeling anxious when your relationship partner learns new things about you.

Actions: Actively hiding truths from your relationship partner. Pretending to be things you aren't because it's "easier."

Reflect and Act

Reflect: What are all the different parts of you, including your aspec identity, that you want seen by your relationship partners? Think about what this means in different kinds of relationships. What does it look like in friendships? What does it look like in familial relationships? What does it look like in other intimate relationships?

Act: You are your most important relationship partner, so the respect and recognition you give yourself is instrumental in building it with others. Write a letter to yourself, celebrating all the things you value most in who you are as a person. Celebrate your accomplishments. Celebrate your identities. Tell yourself all the things you want to hear from the people in your life. Be your own cheerleader. Then, if you are feeling brave, share it with a trusted friend...or a few. Return to this letter when you need reminding of what being seen means to you.

TOOL #10: CARE

The final tool in our Relationship Toolbox is the one I consider the most important: care.

Care is the practice of extending ourselves in the pursuit of providing for the health, welfare, and protection of someone else. Care is the choice to use our resources, in all meanings of the word, to attend to the needs of the people we are in relationship with.

Care is about action

We think and talk about relationships most often through the lens of emotions. We focus on the emotions that relationships bring to us—love, safety, happiness, and all the good vibes in that emotional neighborhood. We locate the issues in a relationship in the emotions we don't want to have, such as anxiety, frustration, anger, and fear. We measure the rising and falling temperatures of our relationships against the ebb and flow of our emotions. Relationships begin because we feel a lot. Relationships end when we stop feeling anything.

This is not to say that emotions don't matter when it comes to relationships. They do. They matter a lot. But what we feel has a tough time reaching past our own borders. Our feelings touch us, but they don't touch our relationship partners. I can love my husband, for example, but the act of my feeling love for him doesn't really do much for him tangibly. That love is in me. It's a thing I experience. And in order for him to experience it, I've got to do something with it.

That something is care. Care is the shape our emotions take when they're turned into action. Care is a thing we *do*. Care takes the things we feel about our relationship partners and manifests them into things our partners can feel. It's why I use the word "extend" to talk about how we share ourselves in care. We take what's available in us and extend it outward to include our relationship partners. Sometimes that means literally bringing our bodies together, in a hug, a kiss, a cuddle, or sex. Sometimes that means using our body to support our partners, in making dinner, doing the laundry, planning a fun day trip, sharing a hobby. Sometimes it's simply being actively present for our relationship partners, in reassuring, affirming, sharing our vulnerabilities, holding safe space for theirs, or simply just deeply listening.

Every kind of relationship we have benefits from care. In every form of connection we share with other people, *doing* is important. We may undertake different degrees of doing, depending on the nature of the relationship and how we've committed ourselves in that relationship. But there's no relationship if we aren't actively showing up.

Our emotions can be mercurial. But our *actions* have shape and weight and impact.

Care is a choice we make

Care is a choice, a conscious decision we make. The action of care is one we undertake of our own free will.

This facet of care echoes an important facet of other tools we've discussed in this section: it's got to come from us. Care is not something we can provide under duress. It's not something we can provide if we're being forced or manipulated. We can't provide care when we are being lied to or having the truth withheld from us. We also can't force people to accept or receive our care. We can't demand that our relationship partners let us be there for them. We can't twist their arm into embracing things we want to do for them. We can shove our concern and support onto our people, but they're not likely to feel very good about it. We might go through the actions of care under these circumstances, but it won't be *care*.

Care needs to be freely given, informed, specific, enthusiastic, and reversible. Sound familiar? It should. These were all qualities we identified as being essential for consent.

You can think about care as what's provided on the other side of consent. Whatever is necessary for consent to be given is also necessary for care to respond to it. If we consent, say, to physical intimacy with our partner, we should expect the physical intimacy we receive to be as thoughtfully considered. If we consent to one night a week hanging out with a friend watching horror movies, then we should expect our time and space to be honored as such. If our relationship partner consents to a conversation about some anxieties that have come up, we should respect that subject and not tack on three other issues out of the blue.

Care, in both directions, has more weight, more value, more depth, and more power when it is a freely given, enthusiastic choice. When they are in need, of all the things we can do in the world—and there is so much we can choose to do—we choose to give of ourselves to support our relationship partner. That's what care looks like when it is at its best.

Why care is important for aspec folks

As aspec folks, along with every other person under the overarching queer umbrella, we move through a world that denies us care. The systems that govern our world don't account for our needs. The messages that pervade our world call us sick, broken, immature, afraid. Laws get made that actively ignore or harm us. The media doesn't depict us or give us equal space to tell our own stories. Our communities only support us when we follow social scripts that aren't made for us. Everywhere we turn in the world sends a single, clarion message: "The care we have to provide is not for you."

To be aspec and demand care is a revolutionary act. To be aspec and provide care is a revolutionary act. To stand in the face of a world that refuses to imagine us and say "I am here. I deserve care. And I will still *give* care in the absence of receiving it" is a powerful assertion of our validity, our worth, and our possibility.

And when we care for each other—as fellow aspecs, as fellow queers, as fellow human beings—that care knits together the fabric of a better and more inclusive world. When we don't turn away from each other, when we give of ourselves, and when we graciously receive what others choose to give to us, we're building the world we *deserve*.

That's the power of care.

Reflect and Act

Reflect: What have been some meaningful examples of care others have shown you? How did those experiences make you feel? What have been some meaningful examples of care you've shown others? How did those experiences make you feel?

Act: A great way to practice care is to practice it in community with others. Organize an act of community care with friends, family, or other members of your human network. Maybe it's collecting food for a local food bank. Maybe it's gathering donated books for the LGBTQ center's library. Maybe it's cleaning up the neighborhood sidewalks on a weekend afternoon. It doesn't matter if there are 20 of you or just two of you. It doesn't matter if the action is large or small. What matters is working together to actively provide care to people in your community.

PART TWO

The Relationship Workshop

A Reminder Before We Get to Work...

N ow that we have a fully stocked set of relationship tools, it's time to put them to use in the creation of safe, healthy, and affirming relationships.

This part of the book is called "The Relationship Workshop" for a reason. "Workshop" is how I see the space we occupy in building relationships. It's a constructive space, a building space. It's not a space where relationships simply happen; they require effort, focus, and work. It's not a space where relationships simply grow; they require our choices and presence in order to find a form that works. It also places the agency and power where it belongs: in us. We are the architects of our human networks.

The six chapters that make up this part of the book explore the ways we put our Relationship Toolbox to use and how we can live out, through a variety of lenses, "A New Kind of Perfect" (ANKOP) relationships. Let's refresh ourselves on the four central ideas of an ANKOP relationship:

1. Love and sex do not make a relationship real, valid, or valuable. They can be part of what people want and pursue in a

relationship, but they are not essential to a relationship working or to a relationship mattering.

2. The outcomes of a relationship—whether it ends in marriage or produces children, for example—do not make a relationship real, valid, or valuable. They can be part of what people want and pursue in a relationship, but they are not essential to a relationship working or to a relationship mattering.

3. Hierarchies do not make a relationship real, valid, or valuable. We do not need to devalue or dismiss one kind of relationship in order to make another kind feel important. All relationship types are whole and worthy of prioritizing within themselves.

4. What makes a relationship real, valid, and valuable is determined by the people in the relationship, collaboratively and consensually. No relationship built with respect and care for the wholeness of the people in it should be seen as broken, wrong, or lacking.

We'll explore ANKOP relationships through six lenses: relationship beginnings, platonic connections, sex, romance, nontraditional forms of relationships, and relationship endings. We'll also explore some relationship structures that aim for unknown horizons. Throughout these chapters, we'll become master craftspeople, crafting affirming relationships to help us thrive.

Chapter 6

How Relationships Begin

One of my favorite bits of humor about the aspec experience is talking about The PowerPoint.

You know The PowerPoint. You're out in the world, maybe at a party, and you meet someone new. They're pretty cool. You're getting along. You've got a ton in common. And you're feeling like this could be the start of a relationship of some kind. You feel comfortable with this person, so you casually mention something that reveals you're ace.

"Ace?" they say. "Like 'asexual'?"

You confirm.

"Oh, I don't know anything about that," they say. "Soooo, what's 'asexual'?"

And the moment has come. The hour is upon you. It's time to haul out The PowerPoint, the long-winded, detailed explanation about what our identity is, how it works, what we do, what we don't, what people believe about it that's just a myth, and what the identity means for us in particular. It's the moment we slap on our educator hat, because sometimes our aspec identities require us to teach a semester of Gender and Sexuality Studies just to get to the end of a party.

The PowerPoint is, of course, an exaggeration. But a lot of folks in the ace and aro communities relate and get a good laugh over it. It speaks to a common problem we face when we're at the start of new connections. Many people who are not ace or aro haven't heard much about our lives and experience. They're coming into relationship with us with barely any background. And we know, as ace and aro folks, that explaining aspec experience is a challenge, one made more complicated when the people we're trying to explain it to hold more stereotypes and misconceptions than basic facts.

The PowerPoint is also a reflection of the anxiety aspec people face around encountering aphobia at the start of new connections. It's so easy for someone who doesn't know much about our communities and experiences to invalidate and dehumanize us, even unintentionally. From microaggressions—"You'll meet the right person one day!" or "Well, maybe you should schedule a doctor visit to get your hormones checked"—to a more aggressive, hateful aphobia that rejects even the existence of ace and aro people, we haul out The PowerPoint at the start of new relationships in an attempt to head these unpleasant experiences off at the pass.

While we aren't quite able to completely ditch The PowerPoint, there's a lot we can do with the relationship skills we've learned and the new expectations we've set for our ANKOP relationships to start in ways that more deeply affirm our aspec identities. This chapter will look at some of those ways, and it will explore some of the mental shifts we can make to better position ourselves for self-confidence and self-advocacy as aspec folks at the start of any relationship.

Let's talk about disclosure

Disclosure is when we share something personal and true about ourselves with someone else, especially when that thing is hard to share. Sometimes it's hard because it's been kept as a secret. Sometimes it's hard because it's something other people wouldn't expect to hear. And sometimes we simply carry fear and anxiety about what the response will be when we share our truth, because we feel it has weight and consequence.

That's why I use "disclosure" when I talk about ace and aro folks revealing their truth to others. We feel incredible pressure when sharing our ace or aro identity with someone new: the pressure of possible rejection, the pressure of being placed in a position to educate, the pressure of facing someone's aphobic microaggressions. We can't simply share our aspec selves with the same ease as sharing our favorite movie or preferred hobby. We have to weigh a number of possible consequences with whether or not we have the capacity to deal with them. *That's* the weight of disclosure.

So I talk about this part of forming new relationships as disclosure, because I think that weight is important to acknowledge. I think it's important to recognize the sometimes difficult calculus aspec folks have to do when sharing their authentic selves with someone new. It's a process that comes with risk. It's a process that can bring pain. So we will think about it and walk through it with a great deal of compassion and care.

When is the right time to disclose my aspec identity with someone new?

Unfortunately, this question has a maybe unsatisfying answer.

The right time to share your ace or aro identity with a new friend, colleague, or relationship partner is when *you* feel ready to share it. Not a moment before.

Remember autonomy? This is your autonomy at work. *You* get to decide when someone knows something important about you. *You* get to decide when you make that investment in another person. *You* get to decide when you give the gift of your authenticity to someone else.

This holds true for all kinds of relationships. The rules don't change because someone is entering your life as a romantic partner as opposed to a friend. You don't owe someone your truth sooner because they're a friend and not a coworker. The nature of the relationship doesn't change the fact that disclosure should happen in your own time. Period.

Our disclosure is a gift

You might be thinking to yourself, "Okay, but don't I owe this to other people?"

Let's dispel this myth right here, right now.

When we enter into relationships with the mindset that our disclosure is something we owe other people, we are seeing our authenticity as something not entirely ours. We are saying that others have some implicit ownership over us, that we aren't always entirely our own.

This is false. We are *always* our own. And in every new relationship we enter, we should see disclosure as a gift, not an obligation.

Sharing our truth is a gift we give someone else.

No person is owed a gift. No person can walk into your house, take something of yours that's valuable, and say, "Well, you owed me this." Your truth is precious, and you get to decide when it's shared and who's worthy of sharing it.

So what do we owe other people? We owe them fair consideration. We owe them the fulfillment of the commitments we make to them. We owe them clarity of our intentions. We owe them the courtesy of not misleading them about what we commit to in relationship with them. We owe them the respect to communicate when conditions within ourselves or between us change.

But isn't withholding the same as lying?

You'll hear plenty of allo folks, particularly if we're talking about romantic and sexual relationships, say things like "You need to say up front, right away, if you're ace or aro!" "You're lying if you don't disclose right away!" "If you don't say it right away, you're tricking us!"

You'll hear this from some aspec folks, too. They'll insist that if we don't disclose up front, right away, we're being unfair and deceitful, taking advantage of the people we're entering relationships with.

Of course, it's important that we don't lead people on. It's important that we don't set up expectations that we know we are unable to meet. We should never commit to things at any level we know we are unable to fulfill. *This* behavior is unfair. When we actively participate in the construction of a false picture of ourselves for others, we're not treating people with care or respect.

But we aren't responsible for people's assumptions. If someone assumes we are allosexual or alloromantic, if someone assumes sex or romance will be part of the deal by being with us, if someone assumes what we desire and how we will express that desire, if someone assumes what potential outcomes exist from a relationship with us without including us in that discussion, the responsibility for those assumptions rests on them.

We are responsible for setting clear expectations and boundaries, doing what we say and communicating as clearly and authentically as we can. That can be done fairly and compassionately while maintaining our autonomy over our ace or aro identity disclosure.

How do we know when it's "the right time"?

There are a few questions we can ask ourselves to help us determine when we've reached "the right time" to disclose.

Does this person feel safe to me? Safety is important, regardless of the kind of relationship we're developing. Do I trust this person to be kind? Do I trust this person to be respectful? Do I trust this person to honor my privacy and honor whatever boundaries I have? Even if they are very close to us—as close as family—and they do not feel safe, we should not feel obligated to disclose if we aren't ready. We don't betray ourselves or our identities when we prioritize our safety.

Does this person need to know? It's not required that every facet of our queerness be available to every person, all the time. Sometimes even people who are safe and trustworthy just don't need to know. Our aspec identity isn't necessary for the relationship we have with them to thrive. It's okay if we choose not to disclose, as long as not disclosing doesn't hinder us from showing up fully and honoring our commitments.

Do I want to invest in the connection I have with this person? Not all relationships carry the same weight and importance. A person we meet at, say, a gaming meet-up who never crosses our path again and the person we really click with at a party and want to continue hanging out with don't hold the same value in our lives. So we don't owe both people the same amount of investment, and we don't owe both people the same kinds of disclosure. We shouldn't feel pressured to disclose in situations when the connection isn't one we want to invest other parts of ourselves in.

Does not disclosing hinder me from developing this relationship authentically? In my experience, this has been the most helpful signpost for when it feels right to disclose. At the very start of all relationships, there's a phase where we can be authentic and present without giving everything away. Think about first coffee dates or the first shift on a new job with coworkers or accidental meetings at a party. We don't tell *everything* in those first encounters with someone new. (Can you imagine how emotionally draining it would be if we did?) We open up parts of our lives in relationships as those parts become necessary for our relationship partners to see us authentically. This goes for our aspec identity as well. If not disclosing is making it hard for you to show up honestly and is making it hard for your relationship partner to see you fully, it's probably time to disclose. It brings us back to the importance of recognition and learning to identify when our aspec identity becomes integral in experiencing recognition.

Our aspec identity is a place for creativity

A mindset that creates anxiety around disclosing our aspec identity at the start of new relationships is the belief that disclosure will be a source of friction in our budding connections. The friction might be small and manageable, like the discomfort of answering questions or explaining ourselves. The friction might be bigger, like the cuts of microaggressions or more direct invalidations of our ace or aro selves. The friction might be significant, like verbal attacks or outright rejection. And the friction can go to the extremes of violence or assault. We can see our aspec identity as the connective thread across these possible outcomes, so we can train ourselves to think of it and the sharing of it as the place where those outcomes live.

But that's just being self-protective, right? That's just being vigilant. *Realistic*.

In Chapter 3, we discussed the balance we have to strike between autonomy and intimacy. That balance is important here. Yes, being aware of the possible negative outcomes our disclosure could create is important in keeping us safe and healthy. But leaning too far in that direction—seeing our identity as the home for those problems—robs us of the kind of emotional intimacy we can create with people we care about.

Our identity is not where friction arises in our relationship. Our disclosure is not the cause of negative outcomes. *Other people's response to the truth of who we are is the problem*. Whether that be at the interpersonal level—an individual person's misconception about aspec lives—or at the very broadest level—the normative and cultural structures that are upheld by institutions and the structures we inhabit—being who we are is not the cause of the pain we experience because of it. Misconceptions are. Lack of education is. Normativities are. Lack of empathy is.

So what do we do about this pervasive mindset? We think of our aspec identity as a place for creativity.

Instead of being the location for frictions like hurt and rejection, our aspec identity can be the space for creation. With each new person we engage with in relationship, our aspec identity—how we hold that identity in our bodies, how we express it with our bodies, how it shapes the way we think, how it impacts what we desire in our connections to other people—offers an opportunity to craft a kind of relationship that affirms us. In a world where relationships often are constructed to erase us, we can ask for something different. We can shape something different. The power to do that lies in our aspec identity.

No apologies!

Raise your hand if you've said any of the following (or something like it) when a new relationship is forming:

- "I know it's hard to deal with, but I'm asexual."
- "I'm aromantic. I know that's hard to understand."
- "I'm sorry for asking for your time. I know you've got a boyfriend now."
- "I know it's challenging to date someone asexual/ aromantic, but..."
- "I'm sorry I'm so confusing."

There are so many ways we've been conditioned to apologize for our aspec identities. The world and other people ask for a lot. Apologize for complicating intimacy! Apologize for not following dating norms! Apologize for wanting time when you don't want to head up the Relationship Escalator! Apologize for being something that doesn't fit readily into my understanding! The variations go on and on. But the common thread is a simple one. We are taught that being aspec is a burden to people who aren't, and if we want their relationship investment in us, we need to be sorry for the trouble we cause.

Being aspec does not require an apology. You do not have to apologize for who you are and what you want.

When we apologize for our aspec identities at the start of new relationships, two important things happen. First, we deepen the negative thoughts we hold about our own identities within ourselves. That apology we make to a friend or family member or dating partner is an echo of the message the world has about us. That apology reinforces normative stereotypes and ideas about us. When we apologize, we allow those untruths to burrow a little deeper into us, and that shapes our self-confidence and self-image negatively.

Second, that apology teaches our relationship partner how to treat our aspec identity. In all of our relationships, we are the most important model for how to affirm and uplift aspec people. Our relationship partners, on average, don't have very much experience in proximity to our lives. They're looking to us to know how to treat aspec experience. So if we apologize and treat our identity as a burden, that's a signal to them that they can do the same. If we treat our aspec identity as an obstacle, that's how they'll treat it.

Go into every new relationship, regardless of type, with a "no apologies" policy. And make it a mandatory one. Don't apologize for being ace or aro. Don't apologize for the things you want from other people. Don't apologize for things they don't understand.

You have nothing to apologize for.

Don't make rejection a self-fulfilling prophecy

I've been married to my husband Neil for almost ten years now. We'd been married four years when I came out as asexual, so at first I didn't have to worry about "dating while ace." But we are polyamorous, and, eventually, I did start dating. And dating as a newly out asexual person held some surprises for me I didn't expect.

Chief among those surprises was a new booming voice in my head showing up any time I made a connection I liked. "Sure, you're having fun now," this voice would say, "but he's going to leave you because you're ace." Or it would say, "You might be enough now, but you know you can't be enough for the long haul. Eventually, you're going to be replaced." I'd try to shake it off, but the voice was persistent. At every turn, it would creep in to remind me that no matter how well things were going, the end was coming. And it was coming because I was ace.

Wanna guess how many of those relationships worked out? (Spoiler: none.)

That booming voice wasn't just chiming in for dating situations, either. It would show up when my asexuality would come up in new friendships. "Hide it," the voice would say, "or they're not going to want to have anything to do with you." It would show up at work. "If you share that you're asexual," it would say, "the whole way they interact with you is going to change, and it's going to be a nightmare to work here."

I spent a long time after coming out as ace believing that rejection was the ultimate endgame of every new connection. Maybe now, maybe later, but always, inevitably, rejection. Not only is that a miserable way to engage in relationships—you're always holding your breath and bracing for the worst—but it becomes a self-fulfilling prophecy.

If you're always bracing for rejection, you're less likely to lean into intimacy while leaning too heavily into your autonomy. You may set boundaries that are more rigid than healthy. You may tend toward less open and vulnerable communication. You may be reluctant to trust your relationship partner. You may find yourself not feeling recognition from your partner, and you may have a hard time offering that feeling of recognition to them.

Engaging from the expectation of rejection may feel like protection, but it actually keeps fulfilling connections at a distance. It cuts us off from pathways to softness and vulnerability, which are necessary for building strong relationships.

Insofar as we are able, we should not assume rejection is the inevitable result of our vulnerability. We should not assume rejection is the only fate awaiting us. Is rejection possible? Of course. It is in all situations where we choose to share ourselves with others. But it is one outcome out of many that are possible. It's not the only option on the table.

How do I introduce my boundaries to a new relationship partner?

An essential part of starting any new relationship, no matter the kind, is establishing our boundaries within that relationship. This is important for two key reasons. First, it makes very clear the space within which this relationship will be built. It outlines what's within your expectations and what is without. It supports the choices you'll make about consent so that they're understandable to your relationship partner. And it helps a relationship partner avoid overstepping or causing harm, since they know with clarity what's in bounds and what isn't.

Second, it helps you build toward an ANKOP relationship. Will most of the people we engage with across our lives understand intuitively how to build relationships that affirm our ace and aro identities? Nope. Odds are, most won't. We'll most often build relationships with folks who are leaning on normative scripts for building relationships, scripts that exclude and erase us. When we establish our boundaries upfront, we're helping to articulate the shape of ace- and aro-affirming relationships. We're saying, "Here's what is in and out for me, and these boundaries are part of relationships that make me feel safe and seen."

Our boundaries articulate the role romance or sex plays in fulfilling relationships. Our boundaries deprioritize normative outcomes such as marriage or kids. Our boundaries can communicate our expectations and wishes around where we fit into the hierarchies of other relationships connecting to this one. And they say, "This is what I want to build, because this kind of relationship affirms who I am. I hope it affirms you as well."

Here are a few tips on effectively and supportively introducing boundaries to a new relationship partner.

Talk about boundaries outside of times you need to exercise them. If you want to ensure your boundaries are heard and that you're in the best place to communicate them clearly, ask your relationship partner for a set time, apart from any kind of boundary negotiation, to talk about them. "Hey, I'm really enjoying hanging out with you. Our friendship means a lot to me. I wanna share with you some of the boundaries I have, so we can keep growing our friendship." Or "I think our relationship is progressing nicely. I want it to keep developing, so can we grab coffee and talk about some boundaries of mine that will impact the next stages of our relationship?" A set time with a set goal in a context that isn't fraught with in-the-moment negotiation will ensure you can do the best communicating possible. You'll have to introduce some boundaries in moments where they're being tested or crossed, of course. But if you can talk about them outside of those moments, you lay some solid groundwork for having fewer of the tense talks.

Treat boundaries as gifts, not demands. Don't treat your boundaries as a list of demands. Arriving at a conversation with a relationship partner and offering your boundaries as edicts or instructions won't feel generous and doesn't embody a collaborative spirit. Relationships shouldn't be dictatorships. Treat your boundaries as gifts to your relationship partner. They're a gift of information about you. A gift of trust in them to honor and respect those boundaries. A gift of recognition by seeing them as someone worth sharing boundaries with. When we offer our boundaries as a gift, we're saying to our relationship partner, "I'm excited about the possibilities of building this relationship with you. Here are some things you need to know about me so we can build the best relationship possible."

Share. Listen. Build. Think of these conversations as a three-step event. Share your boundaries clearly and generously. Listen to the questions your relationship partner might have and to their boundaries that are relevant to yours. Build a collaborative set of boundaries that honor the needs of both of you and the needs of your relationship. This is what we're aiming for: relationships that take the shape of the safety, health, and happiness of everyone in them.

The peril of wearing someone else's hat

While some aspec folks may choose to pull away and guard themselves at the start of new relationships, there's another equal and opposite approach that can also get us into trouble: wearing someone else's hat.

I don't mean a *literal* hat, of course. I'm talking about the adoption of behaviors and attitudes that aren't our own, putting on the appearance of someone we're not. When we enthusiastically show up in a new relationship pretending to enjoy things we don't really enjoy, engaging in behaviors and intimacies that aren't what we want, saying things we don't believe, or committing to things we know we aren't able to fulfill, we're putting on someone else's hat. And that bit of fashion doesn't suit us.

The instinct is understandable. As ace and aro folks, we can experience rejection more often, and rejection *sucks*. It can feel as though the only thing causing us to experience that rejection—and, by extension, all that's preventing us from experiencing someone's care, intimacy, and recognition—is our asexuality or aromanticism. It's the one wall standing in our way. Why not just take down that one little wall?

That one little wall is a load-bearing wall. It's one of the walls holding up the house. Our sexual or romantic orientation is one of the fundamental ways we experience ourselves and the world. It shapes what we experience within ourselves and with other people we form connections with. Beyond that, the way our sexual or romantic orientation is located in the hierarchies of cultural and societal constructs impacts our experience in the world. The truth of us is doing a lot of heavy lifting. Why would we suppress it and cause even more labor?

At the start of new relationships, wear your own hat. And wear it proudly. If the person across from you doesn't like your hat, so be it. If they decide to find someone else with a different hat, that's on them. When you're feeling that pull to hide who you are or pretend to be what you're not, remember: change the *relationship*. Don't change yourself.

Your hat looks *great* on you.

Be where you are. Meet them where they are

Relationships of all kinds are very exciting at the start. It's called New Relationship Energy (NRE), and it's that rush of heightened feelings we get when we're developing a new connection. Most often, you'll hear NRE being talked about in terms of sexual or romantic feelings, but you can have NRE over platonic connections, too. Whenever the beginning of a relationship is filled with big, exciting feelings that make us want to focus a lot of energy and time on that relationship, we're feeling NRE.

One thing NRE does extremely well (it's kind of its superpower) is give us permission to put our expectations on hyperspeed. When we're feeling excited about someone new, we can let our expectations spin out of control. "This relationship is GREAT! I'm gonna spend all my time with this person. We're gonna make plans. This is gonna be a relationship that lasts. Maybe together forever? Maybe! I can't wait to introduce them to everyone. I wonder what kind of furniture we'll get together?"

Exaggerated? Maybe a little. But NRE can easily put our brains and our hearts firmly in the future instead of smartly in the present. Flying into the future on the back of some NRE might feel exhilarating, but it lowers our defenses around things that are important. If we're spinning on good vibes, we're not tending to our personal resources thoughtfully. We might lean too far away from practicing our autonomy. We may overstate our commitments. We may miss red flags in communication or trust.

So be where you are. Meet them where they are. We can feel the thrill of NRE, but we can balance it with our awareness and focus on the present. What are my needs in this relationship right now? What needs my attention outside of this relationship right now? Who am I right now, and what am I bringing into the relationship at this moment? Who is this new person right now, and what are they bringing into the relationship at this moment? What do they need? What needs do they have outside of this?

You're less likely to deprioritize your needs as an ace or aro person if you stay grounded in the present. And you're less likely to ignore situations that don't honor or affirm your aspec identity as well.

Utopia

While it's important to not let NRE get us all caught up in the future, there is one context in the building of new relationships where thinking and dreaming ahead is a good thing.

In the introduction to his book *Cruising Utopia: The Then and Now of Queer Futurity*, late queer artist and scholar José Esteban Muñoz presents what I believe is a really beautiful idea of what queerness is. Muñoz describes queerness as something on the horizon, something we have not yet become. Being queer, Muñoz describes, is taking the experience we have as queer people in the present, warts and all, and using it as fuel to drive our dreams of a future. "Queerness is not yet here," the book begins. But we can see it. We can imagine it. And we live queer lives *inside* that imagining.

For Muñoz, queer is something we are always in the process of becoming. Queerness is something we are always creating. He squarely puts us in the driver's seat of that process. *We* are imagining the world we're moving into. *We* are imagining the queerness we want to inhabit.

I love Muñoz's conception because it centers the act of imagining—imagining the lives we want, imagining the relationships we want, imagining the world we want to inhabit. It prizes the way we want to be seen, respected, treated, loved. In this view of queerness, we design the space our aspec identities occupy with our relationship partners, as well as the place we want them to inhabit within us.

This imagining sits in contrast to what we often do now. Aspec people are always asked to reshape our aceness or aroness into the world as it exists now: into our own sometimes-limiting expectations, into society's always-limiting relationship expectations, into social structures and social norms. We don't do much imagining in this present. Instead, we try to fit ourselves into contexts that don't imagine us. And that's definitely to our detriment.

The beginnings of new relationships don't have to repeat the disappointments of the past. They don't have to reinforce the cultural norms that diminish our asexuality or aromanticism. They don't have to be reiterations of relationship norms that want to hide, limit, and render invisible our aspec experience. They can, instead, be a moment for imagining—and building—something different.

You deserve to have the kinds of relationships and the affirming spaces within them that *you* can imagine. What does an affirming relationship look like? What does a safe relationship look like? What does a joyful relationship look like? Whatever you imagine *can be what you ask for*. We can ask for ace- and aro-affirming relationships that aren't just rearranging the deck chairs on the *Titanic* of social norms. We can ask for relationships that celebrate who we are.

The *imagining* is important. The *asking* is important. It's how we build a world that lets us be the best of what we can be.

Reflect

What do your ideal relationships look like? What do they contain? How are they structured? How are they seen by the world? How can you incorporate some of those utopian qualities in the way you negotiate the beginnings of new relationships?

Chapter 7

Platonic Relationships

Small talk with new acquaintances almost always includes some curiosity about what I do for a living. When I say "Well, I'm a writer, content creator, and asexuality educator," that usually necessitates two important clarifications. First, I have to explain what someone my age is doing on TikTok, Instagram, and YouTube. Second, I have to explain that I am an asexuality educator because, yes, I am in fact an asexual person.

That usually leads to "Oh. But you're married, right?" Yes, technically, that is correct. I am married. I have been married to my husband, Neil, for almost ten years. But that's not a complete picture of my relationship landscape. I'm polyamorous, which means I seek out and have multiple relationships of differing types at the same time. And my polycule—a word describing the network formed when my and my partners' different relationships intersect and interact with each other—consists of four people. We call ourselves "The Constellation," and that's how I'll refer to us from here on out.

Here's how it goes in The Constellation. I am married to my husband, Neil. I also have a romantic partner, Scott, who I've been with for two years. My husband has a romantic partner, Daniel, who he's been with for two years, as well. Other than those three stated romantic relationships, no other connection in The Constellation is romantic or sexual.

Daniel and I don't have romantic feelings for each other. We do not have sexual feelings for each other. But I still consider Daniel my partner. We provide each other companionship, emotional support, care, recognition, and a variety of commitments to nurture and sustain our polyamorous family. It's a relationship with similar intentions as the ones I have with Neil and Scott, but it's a relationship without the romance and physical intimacy those relationships contain.

Daniel is a platonic partner. And in the network of relationships I inhabit in The Constellation, it requires the same relationship skills and intentions as my other relationships.

In this chapter, we're going to explore platonic relationships. We'll talk about what they are and how they can fit into our ANKOP framework. We'll talk about friendships and how they can differ from other kinds of platonic relationships. And we'll talk about how, in an amatonormative and allonormative world, we cope when platonic relationships are devalued and deprioritized for sexual and romantic ones.

The nature of platonic relationships

Platonic relationships are relationships that do not contain sexual or romantic features. They can come in a variety of intensities and levels of commitment. So your weekly board game buddies can be platonic relationships in your life, or you can have a primary life partner that's platonic. Platonic relationships can assume a variety of structures and be spaces for the people in them to work toward any number of outcomes. There's just no sex or romance.

But platonic relationships do have other kinds of closeness, other kinds of connection. Platonic relationships can be sources of emotional support. They can be relationships in which we feel safe and cared for. They can be relationships where we feel recognition the strongest. They can be relationships we go to casually, when they're needed, or they can be foundational relationships that include day-to-day practicalities, shared finances, and building families.

Platonic relationships utilize all of the tools in our Relationship Toolbox, no matter what form the relationship takes and no matter how seriously we choose to prioritize it. Autonomy, consent, and boundaries must be asserted and respected. Good communication, commitment, and compromise are necessary for them to flourish. We seek to feel trust, respect, and recognition in platonic relationships, and care must be demonstrated for these relationships to stay healthy.

While relationships that are formed in work or school situations are part of the platonic relationship universe, they include specific power and responsibility dynamics that go beyond our purposes here. In this chapter, we will be focused on platonic relationships in which partners are on a more equal footing: friendships and platonic relationships with more serious levels of commitment. These are not exempt from issues of power dynamics—race, gender, ability, and other intersections are still present and active—but the platonic relationships we'll focus on here are those that are rooted in emotional bonds between people, instead of being rooted in imposed structures like employment.

How we undervalue platonic relationships (and how we can do better)

Among the constellation of possible relationships one can build, platonic relationships are often undervalued.

All of the normative forces we discussed in Part One view platonic relationships as lesser relationships. Allonormativity and compulsory sexuality view platonic relationships as faulty because they do not provide a space for people to express their "natural" sexual attraction. Amatonormativity views platonic relationships as insufficient because they do not provide the love and romance all humans "naturally" crave. Platonic relationships fall short of heteronormativity because they don't move people toward sexually and romantically exclusive man/woman relationships, and without sex and romance, platonic relationships don't stringently reinforce gender norms to heterosexuality's satisfaction. They fail mononormativity because there's no sex or love to be monogamous with. And on the Relationship Escalator, platonic relationships are viewed as being at the bottom, the relationships we step onto and over in order to move up the escalator towards "meaningful" and "mature" relationships.

This grounds several attitudes about platonic relationships that we hold interpersonally. Platonic relationships are often viewed as the relationships one should grow out of in order to have "real" relationships (which are romantic and sexual ones). One is expected to choose platonic relationships to deprioritize when they come into competition and conflict with romantic ones. One is expected to invest less energy, commitment, and time in their platonic relationships to better support things like work, dates, or romantic and sexual partners. And one is expected to resume platonic support and intimacy at the same level when those previously prioritized romantic and sexual relationships end.

We also consider platonic relationships to be more "simple" than relationships that include love and sex. We consider platonic connection "immature"; if the emotions are immature, then the matter of the relationship must be simple, too. We don't imagine platonic relationships as occupying the same space as, say, marriage or long-term commitment. So we don't envision realities where people have platonic partners, or share a house and finances with a platonic relationship partner, or build families with someone they have platonic affection for. This limited imagination for platonic connection reinforces our negative cultural attitudes.

Platonic relationships are, of course, much more valuable than these social attitudes give them credit for. When we look at platonic relationships through the lens of aspec experience, we see how sustaining and valuable they can be. Platonic relationships can provide ace and aro folks the kinds of relationships that meet their needs without asserting the pressures of love and sex.

Let's consider how platonic relationships answer the values of

ANKOP relationships. Platonic relationships don't contain romance or sex, so they address our value of decentering those experiences in valid and real relationships. Platonic relationships, by their nature, aren't centering the production of romance- and sex-related outcomes like children or marriage, so they meet our value of deprioritizing those. Platonic relationships, when aspec folks either choose to develop them as foundational life relationships or simply choose to emotionally center them, can disrupt the social hierarchies that put romance and sex at the top of the mountain. And without the social scripts of romance, sex, and the relationships we build around those things, platonic relationships can be designed to work for the people in them in whatever ways best suit them.

Rejecting the common social scripts we currently have around platonic relationships and replacing them with scripts that deeply value platonic relationships affirms ace and aro folks and the experiences we inhabit. Platonic relationships can assume many forms. They can be relationships we center, instead of cast aside. They can be relationships we grow and nurture, instead of relationships we grow out of. And they can represent mature, complex, and deeply felt connections between people that are every bit as affirming and real as any other kind of relationship.

Aspec folks and platonic relationships

So what kind of aspec folks choose platonic relationships?

Aroace folks—those who find themselves on both the asexual and aromantic spectrums—can choose to center and prioritize platonic relationships, particularly when their lived experiences of both identities exclude romance and sex. This can look like an aroace person focusing on maintaining very strong friendship circles and investing deep care in those friendships. Or it can look like an aroace person who centers and prioritizes the building of platonic relationships that assume the role of primary life partner. Or it can look like an aroace partner choosing to develop multiple platonic relationships that are knit together in an intentional family where everyone shares responsibilities typically associated with life partners. In all of these scenarios, platonic relationships allow an aroace person who is not interested in including romance or sex in their relationships to build the sustaining relationships they desire.

Would folks who are only either ace or aro ever choose platonic relationships? Absolutely. Developing strong friendships that assume central places in an ace or aro person's life can be sustaining. And for ace and aro folks who build polyamorous relationships—like the ones I am in—platonic relationships may be built with a partner's partner in ways that provide fulfilling kinds of support as well. Or a platonic relationship could simply be a central relationship. Being alloromantic while ace or allosexual while aro does not mean one can't build and prioritize platonic relationships. (There are gray areas, too, and we'll get into those in Chapter 10.)

Okay, but isn't a platonic relationship just a friendship?

No. Platonic relationships aren't "just a friendship." And there are two important things to unpack in this idea.

First, let's talk about friendships and their relationship to platonic relationships in general.

We culturally lump all relationships that aren't sexual or romantic together as "friendships." But that lumping together undermines the complexity of both friendships and platonic relationships. Friendships can fall under the umbrella of platonic relationships because they can and often are relationships that do not contain romance or sex. But some friendships can include sex within their parameters without moving into romantic territory or taking on the functions of primary life partners. In the same spirit, platonic relationships can exist in the more casual and free way that friendships can operate. But some platonic relationships can be built to contain all the complexities, emotional closeness, and practical entanglements of primary life partners. They just don't contain romance or sex. Strictly equating platonic relationships with friendships robs both of their flexibility and complexity.

It's also important to address the "just" in "just friends." Beyond missing the subtleties of friendship and platonic relationships, our cultural attitudes toward friendships belittle their importance. Friendships, and by extension the platonic relationships they're lumped in with, are seen as "relationship lite," cute little relationships we cut our teeth on as children or young adults so that we can learn how to have adult relationships like long-term commitments and marriage. Friendship is treated like the training wheels of relationships: when we get our balance, we can discard them and never think of them again.

This is the Relationship Escalator at work, placing relationships into hierarchies. "Just friends" reinforces the normative idea that romantic and sexual relationships are the relationships we're built for and the ones we should work toward. But friendships and platonic relationships of all shapes are not stepping stones for better, more important relationship structures. They can be deep, nurturing, and foundational.

We should all—ace, aro, *and* allo—treat friendships and platonic relationships with greater respect.

Our words for platonic relationships matter

There's an interesting way we express that "just friends" attitude that's worth discussing here.

We've created an entire language around diminishing the value of platonic relationships. Have you ever heard someone call their friendship a "bromance" or a "womance"? Ever heard someone call a coworker their "work wife" or "work husband"?

We use these words and others like them to describe platonic relationships that are particularly meaningful, platonic relationships that transcend the realm of "just friends" and occupy a more important place in our relationship hierarchy. To denote their importance, they're labeled in ways that make them sound like sexual or romantic relationships: romances, marriage, or the like. They sound cute, but they're reinforcing a negative message about the value of platonic relationships and friendships. They reinforce the message that the only kinds of relationships that deserve to be placed in a position of importance are those that are romance- or sex-centered.

While it can be fun to dub our friendships or platonic connections in these sillier ways, we can do platonic relationships better service by calling them what they are, and we can use language that is specifically designed to describe platonic relationships, too. The aromantic community developed a specific word for a strong desire to develop a platonic connection with someone: a squish. "Squish" was coined to communicate the platonic version of romantic "crushes," so that folks didn't have to use a romantically focused word to describe something platonic. It, and other terms like it, are ways to demonstrate the value and importance of platonic affection and platonic relationships.

Can a platonic relationship really be the main relationship in your life?

Sure! There's no rule in any rule book saying that the central relationship in your life has to be romantic and/or sexual. But this question brings up some important things we can talk about concerning important, primary relationships.

Let's start by clarifying what we mean by "main relationship." For many people, there is a desire to find and build a relationship that sits at the center of their lives, a relationship that's wound up in the emotional and practical areas of life. So it's not just a relationship that fulfills us emotionally and physically. It's also one that helps us handle all the practical parts of moving through the world: bills, care when we're sick, finding a home, maintaining a home, taxes. Our expectations are that it's usually just the one relationship, and that it's usually just a one-on-one relationship.

Is it wrong to want this kind of relationship? Nope. Not at all. But this is a reflection of normative forces that say we should organize our lives around a centered relationship that is exclusive. (Big bonus if there's romance and sex, everyone's hetero, and you make some babies!)

If you desire a central relationship to organize your life around, know that it can be whatever you want it to be, including a platonic relationship. There is no requirement for the relationship at the center of your life, the one that holds a place of primary importance, to be one that includes romance and sex. This is an ace- and aro-inclusive way of imagining these kinds of relationships.

But it's also ace- and aro-inclusive to imagine lives *without* this kind of relationship at the center. We can design our lives in a number of other ways, still meeting our emotional and practical needs. We can build a network of differing kinds of relationships. We can construct polyamorous families. We can even choose to not center any one or network of relationships at all, treating all the various relationships in our lives as equally weighted and important. All of these forms and approaches can hold affirming space for the way aspec folks want to live and embody their aceness or aroness.

That's a long way of saying, "Yes, the main relationship in your life can be a platonic one." But the message is important. You don't have to be limited to any one way of imagining the life and relationships you want.

How do I get someone to want to be in a serious platonic relationship?

If you're interested in pursuing a platonic relationship that upends some of the notions we hold culturally about them—namely, that they're casual, unimportant connections that are lower on the hierarchy than romantic and sexual ones—there are a few things you can do to make that pursuit confidently.

Be clear about what you want. As with any relationship, it's incredibly important that we do some deep thinking about what we want out of it. If you believe a serious platonic relationship is the kind you're most desiring, then take some time to figure out exactly what that means for you. What does the relationship contain? Where does it fit in with other relationships in your life? Where do you want it to fit in with other relationships in your partner's life? What boundaries do you wish to assert in this relationship? What commitments are you willing to make, and which are you wanting to receive? All of these questions can help you understand fully what you want this platonic relationship to look like. And that understanding will help you communicate clearly to someone what you're asking them for.

Communicate with clarity and confidence. I fully acknowledge that this can be hard. But to give yourself the best chance of building the relationship you want, you have to ask for it clearly and confidently. Articulate the shape and substance of the relationship you want to build to your prospective relationship partner. Use the work you did for yourself to ground that communication. Communicate why this kind of relationship has value to you and why you want to build this relationship with them. Take the opportunity to communicate their value to you and the positive qualities you see in them. And most importantly: communicate what you want *without apology*. There is nothing to apologize for in wanting platonic relationships. There is nothing to apologize for in wanting platonic relationships that reflect qualities of relationships like marriage. Treat what you want with the same respect and care you'd want others to hold for it.

Be prepared for the normative pushback. I'm generally optimistic, but I'm not sending you into the fray unprepared. It's very likely that other people, particularly allo folks whose attractions and desires are upheld by normative structures, will resist the idea of prioritizing and centering a platonic relationship. You may find other aspec folks resisting the idea, too. Even with a ton of personal thought and a clear, confident delivery, what you ask for may be rejected as an option. And it may happen more often than not. This is one of the challenging realities of being aspec. Our relationships and realities, even with the best arguments to the contrary, are seen by others as impractical, inadequate, or impossible. I hate this burden we have to carry. But until our normative Big Baddies are eradicated, it's a burden we're going to have to shoulder. I'm not saying we have to be untouched by it. We can and should feel the pain of it. But the pain shouldn't dictate what we ask for, how powerfully we ask for it, and how we see our own self-worth.

Platonic relationships and normative hierarchies

One of the impacts of normative hierarchies on the platonic relationships we create as aspec folks is their discarding or dismissal when a romantic or sexual relationship is found.

Talk to enough aspec folks, and you'll hear this story told again and again: "I was developing this great friendship/platonic relationship with a person. It was terrific. I was getting fulfillment from it. They were getting fulfillment from it. But then they met someone they were romantically and/or sexually compatible with, and their relationship with me was pushed to the side. Without even discussing it with me! And I was expected to be okay with it and not be hurt, because that's how things are supposed to go."

This can be extraordinarily frustrating and painful, even when the relationships in question are casual friendships. No one wants to feel as though their time, emotional support, and presence are instantly less valuable simply because you don't offer sex or romance. But aspec folks are told this time and time again. Our relationships are great until something better comes along.

We can't control what other people do or the choices they make. Autonomy is important for our relationship partners, too. But there are two things we can do to shield ourselves from this negative impact of normative hierarchies.

Invest ourselves more cautiously. Remember when we talked about the tricky balance between autonomy and intimacy? When we're inhabiting relationships that can be discarded for sexual or romantic ones easily, we should be ever more mindful of that balance. We don't have to wall ourselves off from any and all connection, but we also don't have to give everything, either. We don't have to meet every request or demand. This is important in all relationships, sure. But it's even more valuable when the relationship you prize is less culturally valued by your relationship partner.

Remember it's not about you. The pattern of discarding or devaluing platonic relationships when sexual or romantic relationships arise is not specific or due to you. It's a cultural imperative that's deeply embedded in the way we collectively think about different kinds of relationships. So while it's easy to experience that rejection as entirely personal, it's motivated by something much larger than you. This is not telling you to ignore the hurt or saying that there shouldn't even be hurt. But it is saying that you should not *internalize* this hurt. You should not make this hurt a referendum on your worth.

How do I talk to a relationship partner about being deprioritized for a romantic or sexual relationship?

We are reminded constantly as aspec folks that because we don't want the same things in our relationships, we have less ground to ask for things within the relationships we have. We are taught that because, for example, we're "just friends" with someone, there are strict limits on what we can ask for, what we can express, and what we can share with them.

But that's a construction. Being aspec doesn't relegate us to some second-tier status in our relationships. Being ace and/or aro doesn't mean our concerns should be automatically backgrounded to the concerns of others. We can—and should—feel as though we can express our feelings, our wants, and our disappointments with those close to us.

We can celebrate positive change in the lives of our relationship partners—finding new connections and new relationships is still an awesome thing!—while also holding space for the loss that comes along with change. It's okay for you to ask a relationship partner who's devaluing your relationship for a romantic or sexual relationship to work to balance those things *with* you.

You can begin by sharing that you have a mix of feelings about changes happening within your relationship. Some of those feelings are joyful. Some aren't. Share that you want to sit in the safety of your relationship and maybe find a way to work through them together.

You're not demanding they change their plans. You aren't insisting that *nothing* change in your relationship. You're asking for space to exist as yourself, in your full emotions. You deserve that, particularly with people you've invested a lot in and who have invested a lot in you.

Will the relationship still change? Probably so. The world is still what it is. But at least with this approach, you're taking the space you deserve as a relationship partner and claiming the validity of your hurt. Investing in and advocating for yourself is always valuable.

Our platonic relationships have value

You didn't think I was going to end this chapter on platonic relationships on such a downer, did you?

There's a reason I started this exploration of relationship types with platonic relationships. They're amazing! Some of the best relationships in my life are platonic ones, and they provide me with support, joy, and validation that equals what my romantic and sexual relationships provide.

Your platonic relationships have value. Every squish you have. All the friends you make. Each deep platonic relationship you build. They are all worth celebrating.

So celebrate them. And do not be afraid of asking others to do the same. The way we treat our platonic relationships teaches others how they should hold and view theirs. Be good teachers. Be good platonic partners.

Make the world a more platonic place!

Reflect and Act

Reflect: Think about the strong platonic relationships in your life. What qualities do you most value in those relationships? Are there things that your platonic relationships give you that other relationships don't? Reflect on what you receive from platonic relationships that feel sustaining and important.

Act: While we are encouraged to make an effort to celebrate other relationship forms, we don't often make a point of celebrating our platonic relationships. Make a day of your choice Platonic Relationship Celebration Day. Make a choice to express gratitude for the platonic relationships in your life. Celebrate your friends, your coworkers, your neighbors—any platonic relationship that matters to you. Tell them you value the platonic relationship you have and share some qualities of theirs you particularly admire. Give gifts or cards if you feel inclined. Use this day to acknowledge the value of platonic relationships and the people that make them valuable.

Chapter 8

Sex and Relationships

When I came out of the closet as gay at 18 years old, two important things happened. One, I met James, the first gay friend I ever had. And two, I started experimenting with sex.

"Oh my god, I am so excited for you!" James said when I told him I'd officially come out. "You know who you are. That's awesome. Now everyone else knows who you are. That's awesome, too! Now it's time to get you laid!"

James's enthusiasm was sometimes a little too much for me, but he had a relationship with sex I really envied. He was entirely comfortable with who he was as a sexual person. He loved sex. He wasn't afraid of it. He wasn't ashamed of it. Sex brought him a lot of joy. And it brought James a lot of joy to see the people he loved enjoying sex, too. He was always around to talk his friends through their sexual anxieties, provide answers for their difficult questions, listen encouragingly to the stories of their sexual adventures, and support them when their relationships, sexual or otherwise, were tough. And he took a particular interest in me because I had not had sex yet.

That fact didn't really bother me, though. I was (mostly) okay with the fact I hadn't had sex. I didn't have the same relationship to sex that James had. Sex kind of freaked me out. I just couldn't wrap my head around it. The thought of it made me anxious and made my stomach knot up. And while I could picture the date I'd be having with some guy, and the kissing we'd be doing after the date, and the cuddling on the couch we'd be doing while kissing, when it came to the sex part, my brain just wouldn't process it. I couldn't *imagine* what that part looked like. Or felt like. Or...anything.

"You just need to do it," James said. "Deep end of the pool. Just dive right in there. Everybody's anxious about it when they're doing it for the first time. Trust me, once you do it, you'll *get* it. And you'll wanna get it again."

So I tried it. I had sex for the first time with a friend I trusted and liked. And it was...fine. It was nothing like what James was always talking about. But I figured maybe I'd not found the right person or hadn't done it well. So I tried it more times, with different people. Those times were a range of experiences from fine to not-so-much to please-don't-make-me-do-this-anymore. Again, none of those experiences were like the ones James kept promising me I'd have. But I kept at it, trying sex with a lot of different people, trying a lot of different kinds of sex, throwing in fetish and kink here and there. I was living my full sexual explorer fantasy. But nothing clicked.

"There's got to be something wrong with me," I told James one evening, frustrated and disappointed with myself. "I'm the common denominator here. So the problem's got to be with me. Something's going on with me and sex."

It would be a long time before I figured out what was going on with me and sex. I wouldn't figure out I was asexual until I was 41, more than 20 years after James was my cheerleader through my early explorations of sex. I'd spend those 20-plus years developing a relationship with sex that reinforced my belief that I was, in fact, the problem. In doing so, I created a lot of shame and self-loathing that kept me from loving myself and others as fully as I would have liked.

Many asexual folks share similar stories of feeling the pressure to become sexual beings, exploring sex but never really making it work, and blaming ourselves for not meeting those sexual expectations. But there are other ways for us to build relationships with sex, and those relationships celebrate whatever kind of sex we want to have—even when that includes none at all—while also celebrating the fact that we're aspec.

In this chapter, we're going to explore the different ways sex can fit into our relationships. We'll look at the different attitudes we can have about sex for ourselves and for others. And we will look at how aspec experience can expand our ideas about what sex is and how it might relate to us.

So when you say "sex," what are you talking about exactly?

"Sex" is a word that means different things in different contexts, and it can definitionally include a wide spectrum of activities or a small spectrum of activities, depending on who's doing the defining.

(Have you noticed this is a trend with relationship language? The words we use in this area of human experience—"relationship," "sex," "love," and the like—are all used in sometimes confusing ways and without clear-cut, agreed-upon definitions? It goes to show just how complicated this part of human experience can get.)

We'll start with a common, culturally accepted definition and work our way outward. "Sex" is commonly understood to be the collection of activities we do with a partner or partners that involve touching and stimulating the genitals. In some understandings, this range of activity is very small and specific; for some, "sex" is only describing penetrative intercourse. Other understandings are more broad: "sex" describes penetrative intercourse, oral sex, and any other engaged activity where the genitals are the main event. What gets included in the menu of "sex" depends on what the folks defining it are interested in using sex for. Intercourse-focused understandings of sex are likely more interested in sex's procreative function than anything else. The broader understanding, where intercourse is not the only option on the table, is more likely interested in sex as pleasure, sex as emotional connection, and the like. We could engage in a book-length exploration of just this understanding and why different groups care about those different functions of sex, but for our purposes here, let's take this quick view. If you mention "sex" to folks, they'll likely think you mean "doing something with genitals."

That understanding of sex, even in its broader context, fails to encompass what sex is and can be. There is a vast community of people who are thinking, talking, writing about, studying, researching, teaching, and exploring human sexuality who consider "sex" to be much more than just a thing we do with our genitals. For these folks, "sex" is less a checklist of physical acts and more an experience between two or more partners that incorporates a wide range of physical and emotional intimacies. Yes, it can be "doing something with genitals." But it can mean physical pleasure without genital stimulation. It can be partnered or unpartnered. In a broad way, this version of "sex" is focused on a shared experience of pleasure that includes our bodies in some capacity, without setting strict definitions on what that bodily participation entails. This version of "sex" considers intimacy, pleasure, and connection as essential components, and the ways we get there with our bodies (or sometimes without) can be included in how we understand our sexual selves.

In this chapter, we're going to lean into this second understanding of sex. There are two important reasons why. First, this understanding of sex is broadly ace-inclusive. It allows for individuals across the spectrum of asexuality, regardless of their relationship with genitally focused sexual activity itself, to be included in the conversation. (We'll talk more about why this is important later.) This version of sex allows sex-repulsed folks—folks who have strong negative feelings regarding sexual activity—to be part of the conversation as much as sex-favorable folks—folks who have positive feelings about including sex in their lives and relationships. And second, this broader understanding is inclusive of folks who, for whatever reason, have bodies that are unable to perform genitally focused sexual activity. This may include folks who have disabilities that make genitally focused sex impractical or impossible and folks whose bodies exist in ways that do not permit certain kinds of physical intimacy. Thinking about sex in a way that includes the needs of all kinds of bodies, whether they are aspec bodies or not, is important in breaking down the marginalizing forces of our cultural norms around sex.

Sex and ANKOP relationships

So let's break down how ANKOP relationships think about and incorporate sex.

Love and sex do not make a relationship real, valid, or valuable. In our ANKOP view of relationships, sex is only an option on the table when we're building relationships. It does not determine whether or not a relationship can exist in a particular way. It does not determine whether a relationship is more or less valuable than another. It does not determine whether a relationship is one we center in our lives or not. Sex is just something that can exist in a relationship, *if we choose to include it.* If we choose to exclude it, the relationships we build are just as valuable, just as real, and just as worth our time.

The outcomes of a relationship—whether it ends in marriage or produces children, for example—do not make a relationship real, valid, or valuable. In our ANKOP relationships, we are under no pressure to include sex, because the outcomes of sex don't validate our relationships. We are not pressured to produce children. We are not pressured to prioritize our partner's sexual satisfaction. We aren't even pressured to prioritize our own sexual satisfaction. None of these outcomes make any relationship we're in more valid, more valuable, or more real than any other. If we have sex in our relationships, great. If we don't, also great.

Hierarchies do not make a relationship real, valid, or valuable. In our ANKOP relationships, sex does not assign a higher hierarchical value to a relationship than one that doesn't include sex. Sex doesn't make a relationship more important or more worth prioritizing by simply being in the relationship. If we want to center relationships that do not include sex, we can.

What makes a relationship real, valid, and valuable is determined by the people in the relationship, collaboratively and consensually. In our ANKOP relationships, we derive value and authenticity from whatever we choose to share with our partners. If we choose to share sex with our partners, we are making a valid and valuable choice. If we choose not to include sex with our partners, we are still making a valid and valuable choice. The only thing that bestows value and validity to the relationship we're building is our own decision that this relationship is valid and valuable to us.

Can you have intimacy, connection, and pleasure in a relationship without sex?

One of the most damaging myths that our normative Big Baddies have created about relationships is that only sex can bring intimacy, connection, and pleasure to a relationship. With sex, relationships open up into these powerful, deep, connected spaces where people merge and bond and experience the profoundest of pleasures. Without sex, you can have an okay time, but you're really just friends, and all of those magical connections aren't available to you. Or so goes the myth created by compulsory sexuality, allonormativity, and their pals.

What a limited way of understanding human relationships! As we explored in the last chapter, platonic relationships can be spaces of deep and powerful connection, complete with intimacies that are fulfilling for all involved. But even in relationships with romantic components, you don't need sex to fully experience intimacy. You don't need sex to form deep connections with a partner. You don't need sex to feel and share pleasure.

Intimacy, connection, and pleasure are all things we can define for ourselves within the boundaries and agreements of a relationship.

They are things we can define for ourselves within us. If the kind of intimacy we value the most is intimacy that doesn't include sex, that's great! If we want to center connections that don't include sex, that's amazing! If pleasure for our bodies looks like a lot of things other than sex, then that's what it looks like. Sex is not the only way to develop these experiences with a relationship partner. It's *one* of the ways, sure. But it doesn't hold a monopoly.

Aspec folks who do not wish to include sex in their relationships are told time and time again that they're cutting themselves off from "real relationships." Sex does not make a relationship "real." Our ability to experience intimacy, connection, or pleasure does not hinge upon our experience of sex, particularly of the genitally focused variety. We create those experiences, with our relationship partners, in ways that work for us, for them, and for our relationship.

Can you have love without sex?

While we'll do a deeper dive into the questions of love and romance in the next chapter, let's dispel this rumor right here: you can have love without sex.

If we are talking about the romantic kind of love, know that sex is not a prerequisite for that to exist, nor is it a requirement for it to be maintained or sustained. While romantic love and sex are often bound together for many folks, frequency does not equal necessity. Asexual alloromantic folks exist, and their experience of romantic love is not hindered or erased by the relationship they have with sex. Beyond romantic love—because there is a lot of love to be had beyond romantic love—sex is still not a requirement. Love in whatever form we seek it can be had without including sex in the mix.

How can sex be sex without genitals?

Do you remember in our discussion of the normative Big Baddies, we talked about the Relationship Escalator? That was the normative idea that all relationships could be placed on an ascending hierarchy, with friendships at the bottom and exclusive, committed romantic relationships at the top. The Relationship Escalator assigns arbitrary values to different kinds of relationships, pushing us to work our way "up" the hierarchy, prioritizing certain relationships over others.

Well, we have something similar when it comes to sex. We'll call it the Sexual Staircase, and it's another socially constructed system. It assigns arbitrary values to different kinds of physical intimacy, pushing us to work our way "up" the hierarchy, classifying some activities as "sex" and others as not.

The Sexual Staircase takes a number of the physical activities associated with sex—kissing, cuddling, touching, manual stimulation, oral stimulation, penetration, orgasm—and organizes them into a linear, progressive model that places less value on physical intimacies that are not genitally focused and places more value on physical intimacies that are genitally focused. At the top of the staircase is orgasm, specifically orgasm achieved through penetration (and male orgasm even more specifically, because we're still in a patriarchy, don't forget!), which is considered the ultimate goal of sexual activity. If you reach the goal, you "did a good sex," so to speak.

So while kissing and cuddling and touching may be nice and feel good, they're not considered "real" by the Sexual Staircase. They're a warmup for the "real thing." Activities at the lower end are included only insofar as they facilitate more valuable activities, like oral sex or penetration, but they are not to be considered valuable in and of themselves. According to the Sexual Staircase, in order for sex to be good or complete or valuable, it has to include genitals, it has to include penetration, and it has to include orgasm.

So why do we have the Sexual Staircase? The activities it places the most value on—genitally focused penetrative sex—is the kind of sex, when done heterosexually, that leads to procreation. Society has a deep, abiding interest in its members organizing themselves into sexually exclusive, heterosexual pairs that have sex to produce offspring. The Relationship Escalator exists to push us towards those kinds of relationships. The Sexual Staircase exists to push us towards that kind of sex.

The reality, however, is that none of the activities on the Sexual Staircase are inherently more valuable or more "real" than any other. And none of the activities on any part of the Sexual Staircase make a particular relationship more "real" than any other. All of the activities can be physical intimacies we desire. All of them can be physical intimacies we take pleasure in. We can decide to not desire or take pleasure in any of them and still have full, complete relationships with our relationship partners.

So sex can be sex without genitals when you stop looking at sex as a staircase, and start looking at it more as a wheel. Instead of physical intimacies lined up, step by step, in an arbitrary ascension towards orgasm, physical intimacies are laid out in a circle, sharing equal space, sharing equal weight, and each one as valid an option as another. None are above. None are below. It's simply a matter of where you'd like to spin the wheel. Not which step you want to make your way up or down toward.

Why is this important for aspec folks? What does it matter if we're included in the conversation or concept of sex?

There are two big reasons I think it's valuable for aspec folks (and everyone, honestly) to embrace a broader definition of sex that rejects the Sexual Staircase.

First, not all aspec folks will have the same relationship to sex. Ace and aro experience is not monolithic. What does unite all aspec experience is it being, in some way, non-normative. Some element of your ace or aro experience exists outside of cultural norms of romance and sex. And that reality, no matter where it lies within your experience, is going to show up in the way you experience sex as a part of (or as no part of) your relationships. The broader view of sex, where sex is not a march toward penetrative orgasm but an exploration of physical intimacy and pleasure at one's own speed and desire, includes many of the aspec relationships with sex. If you're a sex-favorable aspec person, plenty is on the table. If you're sex-neutral, you can include what you dig and discard the rest. If you're sex-averse or sex-repulsed, you can prioritize the physical intimacies that don't create negative feelings. The broader view of sex we're holding here makes space for all of those dynamics and sees them all as valid.

The second important value is that this broader view of sex makes space in the conversation about sex for those who want nothing to do with it at all. The Sexual Staircase does more than just assign competing values to different kinds of physical intimacies. It also creates a powerful binary between choosing intimacy and not choosing it. By grouping physical intimacies in a hierarchy, the Sexual Staircase is also implying that there is greater value in choosing intimacy than there is in not choosing it. "Not having sex" is nowhere on the Sexual Staircase. It's not even an undervalued option. It doesn't make the cut, so the message is that "not having sex" is an inconceivable choice, a choice you simply cannot entertain. Being an aspec person who wants nothing to do with sex means occupying an experience the world doesn't even include as an option.

Our broader view does, however, make space for this reality. No choice of physical intimacy is valued more or less than any other. All forms of physical intimacy are weighted equally in relationships. What matters in our broader view is what the people in the relationship desire together, and if that shared desire is "none of the above," then that's as valid as the relationship that chooses "all of the above."

It's a radical view of sex to say that both the couple who's doing "all of the above" and the couple that's choosing "none of the above" are developing healthy sex lives. But a view of sex that includes all aspec experience—even aspec experience that is completely without the forms of physical intimacy that show up on the Sexual Staircase—is a more complete, more accurate view of sex. Not every aspec person will wish to see their intimacy choices that way, and that's okay. But when aspec folks are part of the holistic notion of sex, the possibilities for all people are expanded. The possibilities of sex are expanded.

Sex positivity, sex negativity, and the way we feel about sex for ourselves

This is a good moment to clear up some confusion folks have about a set of terms articulating our attitudes and relationships with sex.

There are two terms that have been coined to speak broadly about the attitudes we can hold about sex as a general concept and sex had by other people: sex positivity and sex negativity.

Sex positivity is a set of values and attitudes about sex that assign no moral weight, good or bad, to any consensual sexual activity between adults, including the consensual decision to not have sex. Basically, sex positivity means you think it's okay if people want to have sex. It's okay, regardless of the kind of sex they want to have. It's okay, regardless of how often they want to have it. It's okay, regardless of who they want to have it with. And it's okay if they don't want to have it at all. As long as everyone's an adult, and everyone's consenting to whatever decision is being made, it's cool. That's sex positivity. It's believing we should neither be pressured nor discouraged from making the informed consensual decisions we want to make around sex.

Sex negativity is a set of values and attitudes about sex that *do* assign moral judgment to sexual activity, even consensual sex between adults. Sex negativity believes sex to be inherently "bad." It believes sex to be something dangerous, dirty, shameful, or wrong. It believes sex to be inherently bad for *everyone*, regardless of the kind of sex they're having, the frequency at which they're having it, and who they're having it with. Sex negativity is a global attitude about the "wrongness" of sex. It's believing that sex is, generally, something we should be ashamed of and something we should avoid.

These two ideas are *general* attitudes about sex. They are attitudes about sex we hold for people generally. They don't necessarily explain the feelings we hold *personally* about sex for ourselves. We have a different set of terms for that.

Sex-favorable describes having positive feelings about sex in your relationships and actively wanting sex to be a part of certain relationships. *Sex-neutral* describes having no feeling, good or bad, about the inclusion of sex in your relationships, where sex can be an option, but there are no strong feelings about it either way. *Sex-averse* describes having some level of comfort with sex and sexual ideas abstractly, but having negative feelings about actually including sex in your relationships. And *sex-repulsed* describes having strong negative feelings about including sex in your relationships in any way, even abstractly. These four terms describe a person's individual relationship to sexual activity. They talk about how they feel about sex *for themselves*. There is no assumption to be made about how a person feels about sex in a more global sense based on the language they use from this set of terms to describe how they feel about sex personally.

This distinction between the words we use for more global attitudes about sex and the words we use for our individual attitudes about sex is important. These terms often get used interchangeably, and when they do, it can perpetuate negative stereotypes about aspec people and sex.

It's often assumed that aspec folks hate sex. It's assumed we hate it for ourselves. It's assumed we hate it for other people. It's a specious stereotype that not or rarely experiencing sexual or romantic attraction equals a hatred for sex. This can lead to a host of negative impacts for aspec folks: microaggressions, rejections, unnecessary pressures in relationships, and, in extreme cases, domestic violence or assault.

There is no monolithic attitude that aspec folks hold about sex for themselves or about sex for others. There is as much diversity of attitude and experience among aspec folks around sex as there is among allosexual and alloromantic folks. You cannot assume, by virtue of knowing someone is aspec, what they feel about sex individually or globally.

Why does this matter? First, we must allow space for aspec folks who are sex-averse and sex-repulsed to hold negative attitudes and feelings about sex for themselves without those feelings subjecting them to judgment or discrimination for their aspec identity. It's okay to be sex-averse or sex-repulsed. It's okay for that personal relationship to sex to be a lifetime constant or to be developed through specific experiences one has, such as sexual trauma. One can feel negatively about sex individually and make the decision to not include sex in any relationships without that meaning one hates sex generally or one judges others who have sex.

It's also important to hold space for aspec folks who are sex-favorable and sex-neutral and who do include sex in their relationships. Sometimes, the stereotype of aspec folks hating sex is used to negate or diminish the identities of sex-favorable and sex-neutral aspec folks. Having sex or being positive about sex is being seen as not being "aspec enough," and these ideas can sometimes even come from other aspec folks. Having favorable relationships with sex does not make someone "aspec-lite" or "trying to be allo." Holding negative attitudes or feelings about sex for oneself personally does not validate one's aspec identity nor does it make one's aspec identity more "pure." Enjoying sex within your own life and relationships and holding sex-positive attitudes about sex for others does not make one less aspec in any way.

It's essential we hold all the ways in which aspec folks relate to sex as individuals and as members of the larger human community. You can be aspec, not want sex for yourself, but still allow supportive space for others to pursue the relationships they want. You can be aspec, seek out sex for yourself, and still hold supportive space for others to pursue the relationships they want. We can make the choices we need and want to make for ourselves, while still being supportive of the choices others need and want to make for their lives and relationships.

Sex for aspecs: sex is more than "sex"

Before we touch on a few practical strategies for navigating sex and sexual intimacy in relationships (if you want to!), I want to clearly articulate three big ideas around sex for aspec folks.

First up: sex is more than "sex."

The normative forces like compulsory sexuality and allonormativity limit the scope of what we think of as "sex." It becomes focused on genitals in the general and focused on penetration when there's a penis involved. And, thanks to the Sexual Staircase, we often equate success with the very limited goal of orgasm. Minus those involvements and goals, we're "not having sex."

For so many aspec folks, having to achieve this limited notion of sex on a regular basis is impossible and/or undesirable. Either there's an inability or disinterest in the genital focus or the penetration focus. Maybe there's a physical level of comfort that's available, but orgasm is a point of repulsion or aversion. This can discourage aspec folks from developing a relationship with "sex" in a broader sense that works for them.

Sex does not have to be confined to these parameters. Sex can include physical intimacy that isn't genital-focused or penetration-focused. Sex doesn't have to prioritize orgasm and doesn't have to consider lack of an orgasm a failure. Aspec folks—and all folks—can imagine and practice sex in any way that works for them. They can define what sex includes or doesn't. They can define what successful sex looks like or doesn't. And they can choose whether any form of sex is going to be a part of any relationship they make.

Sex for aspecs: no sex is part of sex

We culturally think of "no sex" as something separate from "sex." That "no sex" is a negation of sex. That they are separate spaces one can inhabit. You can inhabit the space of sex, which is the space where there is intimacy and connection and closeness with a partner. Or you can inhabit the space where there is "no sex," which is the space where there is none of that, where there is just the absence or maybe only a desire for sex to be present.

We don't have to think of sex in such a strict binary, particularly a binary that erases so many aspec people. Intimacy, closeness, and connection can all exist whether the activities on the Sexual Staircase are present or not. Intimacy, closeness, and connection can exist no matter what kinds of physical intimacies are on the table. "No sex," in whatever configuration or definition of sex one is working with, can contain intimacy, closeness, and connection as much as "sex" can.

This seems like a fiddly distinction to make, but I think it's really important. And it works in tandem with the first idea for folks who have stronger resistances to including sex in their lives and relationships. If sex is supposed to be a space where we use our bodies to create closeness and connection, what does that look like without "sex"? What does time together look like? What does our care and attention look like? How can we wrap "no sex" into our full picture of shared intimacy with someone? How can we honor it, cultivate it, look at it as another tool for us to connect deeply?

"No sex" being a part of sex does more than just make space for aspec folks of every experience. It expands the possibilities of sex and intimacy for everyone.

Sex for aspecs: sex doesn't own desire and pleasure

Compulsory sexuality and allonormativity have many detrimental effects, but one of the big ones is the way they inextricably connect sex with desire and pleasure. The messages of the culture, messages that get echoed by the people around us and our relationship partners, insist that desire and pleasure are exclusively part of our sexual selves. To desire another person is to want to have sex with them. To seek out pleasure with another person is to seek out sex. If we don't want sex with someone, we don't desire them. If we don't want sex with someone, we can't experience pleasure with them. This isn't true in every single scenario, of course, but it is an overarching message that's communicated often.

For aspec folks, this is extremely limiting, both to us as human beings and to desire and sex as ideas. We don't want to be excluded from desire and pleasure. And we don't want to only be a part of someone else's desire and pleasure if sex is involved. We want partners who embrace that we desire them without that desire being sexual. We want partners who find pleasure with us in non-sexual ways that bodies can be together. And we'd like to have a shared space with a partner where we can explore these ideas expansively.

Aspec folks shouldn't be cut off from the experiences of desire and pleasure simply because we choose not to include sex in our relationships. We deserve more expansive ideas of how desire can be felt. We deserve more expansive ideas of how pleasure can be experienced. And both desire and pleasure can be things aspec folks have and enjoy regardless of the way they relate to sex within their relationships.

Advice for aspec folks who want to include sex in their relationships

Here's some advice for aspec folks who do want to include sex in their relationships.

Know what you want. Know what you don't. Just because an aspec person is open to or enjoys having sex, it doesn't mean they stop being aspec. And it doesn't mean they won't have certain feelings or needs around sex that sit outside cultural and societal norms. So it's important to know exactly what you want and exactly what you don't want when it comes to sexual intimacy. You want to confidently articulate your needs, your wants, and your dealbreakers around intimacy to a relationship partner. It's essential for communicating consent. It's essential for setting strong boundaries. A good way to achieve this is to do an intimacy inventory. Think about all the ways one can engage in physical intimacy. Include everything, from the simplest forms of touch like holding hands to the full range of sexual intimacies. Sort them into three categories: "Yes" (things that you are open to, enjoy, and wish to engage in), "No" (things you do not enjoy, are not open to, and do not want in your relationships), and "Negotiable" (things you might be willing to try or explore, but requires conversation and negotiation, and may end up as a "No"). Then share this inventory with a relationship partner. Talk about it. Get them to do an inventory of their own. This eliminates assumptions or confusion about what's on the table for you as an aspec person and for the relationships you build.

Allow for and demand room to change your mind. One thing sex-favorable aspec folks face is the assumption that what we agree to at one point in a relationship will remain true throughout a relationship. But our relationships to sex can undergo evolution and change. What we feel comfortable doing with our bodies can undergo evolution and change. It's important we allow room for that change and not punish ourselves for having evolving feelings and wants about sex. And it's important we demand that room from our relationship partners, too. When they respect that space for change, they're respecting our aspec identity.

Let your relationship to sex be _your_ relationship to sex. Because sex-favorable aspec folks are having sex, their allo relationship partners can assume their relationship to sex mirrors that of an allo person. But aspec folks who are sex-favorable can have relationships to sex that look nothing like allo ones. We may not want it as frequently. We may not be excited about it in the same way. We may feel differently about the way it connects us emotionally to our partners. There are a thousand variables for sex-favorable aspec folks that construct a relationship to sex that will be different from our allo relationship partners. Let those differences be present. Let those differences be valuable to you. Let your relationship to sex be _your_ relationship to sex. You might feel pressure to perform your sexuality differently to satisfy a relationship partner or to satisfy cultural expectations. But try to resist that pressure to perform. Inhabit your body and your wants in the unique way you wish to. Inhabit your sexuality in a way that's authentic to you.

Advice for aspec folks who do not wish to include sex in their relationships

Don't want sex to be a part of your relationships? Here's some advice for you.

Know you can ask for what you want. It's okay to want relationships without sex. It's okay to want relationships that have romance but no sex. It's okay to want relationships that are strictly platonic. It's okay to want relationships that are somewhere in between. You can choose to exclude sex from your relationships and be confident in that choice. Sex-averse and sex-repulsed aspec folks are told all the time that wanting relationships without sex is a brokenness, a flaw, a "wrong" choice. They are often shamed for the kinds of relationships they want, and they're pressured into making different choices. But your desire for sexless relationships is not a brokenness. It's not a flaw. What you want is what you want, and you should feel empowered to ask for it.

Reframe rejection. Pursuing some relationships without including sex—romantic relationships, for example—can be an uphill battle, and that pursuit can often end in rejection. So it's important for aspec folks who don't want sex in their relationships to suit up in a bit of protective armor that helps navigate rejection. When you're rejected for the kind of relationship you want, don't think, "Well, that's more proof that being who I am and wanting what I want is messed up and wrong and bad and shameful." Instead, think, "Yes, they rejected me, but that tells me they can't give me what I need. That tells me they aren't right for what I want. That tells me they aren't right for me." While the ways other people respond to our aspec identities can hurt us, other people's responses are not statements of our worth or value. Other people's responses aren't statements of the worth of what we want. They're just other people's responses. We are always deserving of the lives and relationships we want.

Release comparison. Rejection isn't the only obstacle for aspec folks who choose to exclude sex in their relationships. Comparison proves to be a mighty opponent. We look at ourselves through comparisons to folks who have sex. We look at our relationships through comparisons to relationships that include sex. We assign ourselves value through comparing ourselves to cultural and societal norms. How often do sex-averse or sex-repulsed aspec folks think of themselves as "not enough" or "not worth pursuing" or "not as good as"? We can't see ourselves through the lens of what someone else wants or does or has. Release that comparison. What you are, what you want, what you can bring to a relationship is unique to you and is *worthy* and *valuable*. It is worthy and valuable in and of itself. It doesn't have to measure up to anyone else's expectations or standards. One of the great gifts we can give ourselves as aspec people, particularly as aspec folks who choose to exclude sex and/or romance from our relationships, is to believe in our value *simply because we exist as we do*. We are not in competition with any other way of being. We don't have to look to other ways of being to see our way of being as unique, valuable, and *ours*.

Reflect

What are the different attitudes I hold toward sex? What attitudes do I hold towards sex for myself? What attitudes do I hold toward sex for other people? If I could decide what attitudes and expectations society held around sex, what would I include? What would I exclude? Are there ways to take these ideas and bring them into my relationships?

Chapter 9

Romance, Love, and Relationships

I'm not very good at romance.

I've *never* been very good at it, but many years, many romantic relationships, and plenty of experience in the romance trenches have not appreciably increased my skills in the matter. It might be the case that I reached the pinnacle of my romantic prowess when I got my parents to buy that necklace for Angelica back in middle school.

Lucky Angelica. Not so lucky my husband and partner.

It's not that I don't want to be romantic. I do. I think my partners would very much appreciate it. Particularly because they are *very* good at being romantic, and I'm sure they'd dig getting a little of that reflected. It's more that my brain just doesn't really compute romance. It's a language my brain doesn't speak very well. I'm a tourist in a land of native romance speakers.

It's also that so much of what constitutes capital-R Romance seems kind of silly to me. I don't think that people who are good at it or who enjoy it are silly. I just think the gestures and postures themselves feel silly. Or maybe "silly" is the wrong word. Maybe what I mean is that, with so much of romance, I just don't get why it *works* for people.

Here's a case in point. My husband and I recently celebrated our ninth wedding anniversary. We didn't do anything on the evening of our *actual* anniversary, because I was incredibly sick and was in no mood to be anywhere other than curled up in bed. But a week later, we went out on our Big Anniversary Almost-a-Decade-Married Date—we went to the local independent bookstore, bought a couple books each, then had dinner at Buffalo Wild Wings.

No gifts. No flowers. No cards. No nothing. Just four paperbacks and some wings.

Thankfully, after almost a decade, my husband is cool with my preference for anti-romantic vibes. Because for me, that evening was *perfect*. We hung out, we laughed, we shared space, and we were connected. No further gestures needed, for me. Anything more, anything too frilly or demonstrative or ooey-gooey touchy-feely, would feel like too much.

Now, I am not aromantic. I do experience romantic attraction. And I am not saying my lack of romantic skills is equivalent to being aromantic. It's not. But I offer my experience as a way to suggest that maybe romance and its gestures aren't as fundamental or universal as some cultures make them out to be.

In this chapter, we'll look at romance and love—they're two different things—and how they intersect with the lives of aspec folks. We'll cover some Big Ideas about love and romance, and we'll offer some practical strategies to help navigate building relationships with or without romance or love.

What is romance anyway?

While there's a lot of room to define sex in a wild number of ways, romance is an even trickier concept to define. If you ask most people to define "romance," you'll likely get a slew of different feelings, actions, and beliefs, all swirling around some common themes. It's about love! It's about warm, fuzzy feelings! It's about romantic gestures! It's about flirting! And sure, romance can include all of those things. But if you prod a little further and ask "Okay, but what makes all of those things *romance*?" you'll likely get a shrug.

Probably the most common conception of romance holds that

romance is a feeling. It's the feeling we feel for those certain "special someones." It's a rush of excitement. It's a feeling of warmth and affection. It's a feeling that pulls us into a person. It's a feeling that encourages us to wrap ourselves in them. This conception holds that this feeling is unique and consequential. It's not something we feel for everyone. It's a feeling that comes with people who hold the potential to complete us. Romance is the feeling that signals we might have found "The One." Often, this feeling is called "love" interchangeably with "romance." (We'll get to love a little later in the chapter.)

Is this "romance"? In some ways, yes. This family of feelings can definitely mark the experience of romance. But defining "romance" as simply a suite of emotional experiences doesn't capture the full scope of what romance is and what it does. It's a broader construction with many more tentacles reaching into parts of our lives.

First, romance is strongly tied to the pursuit and acquisition of a long-term life partner. All of the warm, fuzzy feelings associated with romance are attached to notions that those feelings signal the arrival of our (possible) forever mate. When those romantic feelings arrive, it's a signal to differentiate this relationship from the others that don't produce those feelings. And beyond differentiation, we're expected to prioritize the warm, fuzzy relationship over the relationships that aren't. The feelings of romance are functional motivators, as well. Once they've arrived, we want to keep those feelings there. So we engage in actions and behaviors that nurture the continuance of those feelings. The work of cultivating those warm, fuzzy feelings keep us bonded to a partner, or, if we fail to maintain them, lead us to seek out another partner who might be a better fit.

Second, romance encompasses a system of social rituals and definitions for our experience of romantic feelings but also for our hopes to produce romantic feelings in others. Think about the complex world of romance in Western cultures. We label romantic interactions differently from other interactions: "dates" are romantic while "hanging out" is not. We have social protocols (which are very gendered and heteronormative) around asking someone out for a date: the guy should ask the girl, no one else can join you on a real romantic date, the guy should pay, and many more. We have labeled certain gestures like buying someone flowers, getting surprise romantic greeting cards, or writing sweet little love poems for someone as "romantic gestures." With the Relationship Escalator, we've established guideposts for the progression of romantic feelings that take us from first date, to making it "official" as boyfriends or girlfriends, to making it *really* official with marriage. Plus, marriage has its own set of social rituals around what makes a proper engagement, what a wedding ceremony should look like, and how we should celebrate anniversaries. And this is just for Western cultures. Globally, romance looks different depending on what the culture values. Different cultures will produce different social rituals. Different cultures will contextualize and assign different values to the feelings of romance, including assigning little value to them at all.

For our purposes, we'll think about romance in this broader sense. We'll not only see romance as a set of feelings and emotions, but we'll also recognize it as a set of culturally crafted social structures that point us and our warm, fuzzy feelings toward lifelong committed partnerships. And we'll be focusing on Western romantic attitudes and social structures, because those will be familiar to most of the readers of this book. However, as I said earlier, what doesn't speak to your experience is a failure of me and this book, not of you.

When ace and aro folks meet romance

So let's talk about what happens when ace and aro folks brush up against romance.

Aromantic folks who are romance-averse or romance-repulsed face the most intense friction when they brush up against romance. They can be perceived as broken or deficient for not feeling romantic attraction. They can be seen as immature, too anxious, or too scared for not wanting to participate in romantic relationships. And the relationships they do have are often ghosted, dismissed, and deprioritized by their relationship partners when those partners find romantic relationships. This can take a powerful emotional toll on romance-averse and -repulsed aromantic folks, negatively impacting their self-worth, their confidence, and their happiness. Beyond the emotional individual toll, this treatment of romance-averse and -repulsed aromantics is socially isolating. It can be hard to find relationship partners open to the kinds of relationships they seek, and their access to the relationships they do use for support is entirely dictated by whether or not their relationship partners have romantic partners or not. Loneliness, feeling as though they're easily discarded, and feeling as though they're fundamentally unimportant to the people in their lives can be the result.

The challenges don't disappear for romance-favorable and romance-neutral aromantic folks. While they may be open to and seek out romantic relationships despite being aromantic, they're *still* aromantic, inhabiting a non-normative experience of romantic attraction. They can feel as though their aromantic identities are rendered invisible by their participation in romantic relationships. They can be told, "Well, you don't *seem* so aromantic," or "Well, I guess you're not aromantic *anymore*." This can be deeply invalidating. And within their relationships, there may be fluctuations in the comfort level with romance, changes in their individual relationship with romance, or other individual ways of interacting with romance that don't fit normative expectations. Being romance-favorable or romance-neutral is not being "aromantic lite." But these aromantic folks can often be treated this way, and it can lead to frustration, feelings of invalidation, and internalized negative ideas about their aromantic identity.

Asexual folks aren't immune from negative impacts, even if they are alloromantic. Romance and sex are culturally tied together, so for most folks there's no *true* romance without sexual attraction and sex. So even when alloromantic asexuals can walk the walk romantically, if they are sex-averse or -repulsed (or even sex-favorable or -neutral with relationships to sex that upend allo norms), the validity of their romantic feelings can be questioned or denied. Not fitting the sexual norms in our culture can put one's romantic authenticity into question, and asexual folks can find it challenging to sustain romantic relationships, even though they're alloromantic themselves.

Why is this important? Because we often think it's only the aspec folks who are repulsed by romance and who choose to not include romance in their lives that are impacted by amatonormativity and other norms around romance. But *everyone* across the ace and aro spectrums can feel the impact of brushing up against romance.

Romance and ANKOP relationships

Let's look at how our ANKOP ideas shape better relationships for aspec folks around romance.

Romance and sex do not make a relationship real, valid, or valuable. As in our exploration of sex in relationships, we can build real, valid, and valuable relationships that do not include romance. Or we can build relationships that include romance in non-normative ways. But the presence of romance doesn't make any relationship more real. Its absence doesn't make any relationship fake or not worth prioritizing.

The outcomes of a relationship do not make a relationship real, valid, or valuable. In the context of romance, this means things like "making it official," using terms like "boyfriend" and "girlfriend," and seeing marriage as the ultimate form a relationship can take. These are outcomes attached to romance, and while it's fine to desire them, they do not determine the validity and value of a relationship. You can have meaningful relationships without them ending in these romance-attached outcomes.

Hierarchies do not make a relationship real, valid, or valuable. The presence of romance doesn't position a relationship as more important or more worthy of being prioritized. The presence of romance doesn't mean a relationship has "leveled up." And the absence of romance doesn't mean a relationship can be discarded or that it should *expect* to be placed in lower priority to other relationships. We don't need to use romance as a sorting tool for our relationships.

What makes a relationship real, valid, and valuable is determined by the people in the relationship, collaboratively and consensually. A successful, authentic, and whole relationship is one in which the partners in it have thoughtfully and respectfully agreed upon the role romance plays in the relationship. They can decide it plays a big role. They can decide it plays no role. But as long as everyone agrees on the role for romance, they're building a real, valid, and valuable relationship.

But if your relationship doesn't have romance, it doesn't have love. And what kind of relationship is that?

It's time to talk about love.

As we've seen so far, we hold a lot of cultural assumptions about and around romance. But one of the most harmful—and most incorrect—is that romance is interchangeable with love.

"Love" is another one of those words that are used to speak of many different things but then get culturally condensed into a singular association. In the case of love, we assign a wide array of emotions the label of "love." We love the people we marry. We love our families. We love our dogs. We love our friends. We love our job. We love this book or that movie. "Love" becomes a catch-all for a whole slew of affections.

Yet when we talk about *true* love, we mean romantic love. When we talk about the love we should aspire to, we mean romantic love. It's held as the primary form love takes. Every other form is nice and all, but they're all variations of love's realest form, and in many contexts, these varied forms of love are seen as practice for "the real thing."

We cut our teeth on all those other forms of love so we can finally mature and tackle real love in the form of romantic love.

This is why, when aspec folks choose to not include romance in their relationships, it's assumed that no love of any kind can exist. If you don't want the real form of love, the thinking goes, you must not want any kind of love. Or you must not be *capable* of any kind of love. We're only given permission to have full relationships with the spectrum of connection and emotion if we're on board with romantic love as a desire and a goal.

In much the same way as being ace or being aro is just one of the many ways to exist across sexual and romantic orientation spectrums, romantic love is just one of the ways one can experience love. It's not the default from which all other forms are taken. It's just one of the options, one of many. Platonic love, familial love, love of community, love of self—these are all equally valid forms of love. If one chooses to forgo romantic love and prioritize one of the others, it's an equally valid way of organizing your life.

Loveless aros and our norms about love

Since we, as humans, are incredibly resourceful at creating oppressive norms, we not only have norms about which kinds of love are hierarchically better than others, but we also have norms about the experience of love itself.

We believe culturally that the experience of love is a universal human experience. Everyone feels love, and being a human that experiences love is the default human setting. This, of course, gives root to normative forces like amatonormativity and the Relationship Escalator. But it also serves as a way some aromantic folks and well-meaning aro allies justify the validity of aromanticism.

"Sure, aromantic folks may not want *romantic* love. But aro folks can still *love* in other ways!"

This is very well meaning, and it's a sentiment that's true for a lot of aromantic folks. But it isn't *universally* true, and the folks this leaves out have something very important to teach us about our relationships to love and romance.

Loveless aros are folks who not only don't experience romantic attraction but also don't experience or feel connection to love in general. For loveless folks, love isn't on the table at all, regardless of the form it takes. Loveless folks can feel that their lovelessness is rooted in different places. Some feel this disconnection is inherent to who they've always been. Some feel it might be rooted in their experience of neurodivergence or their experience of trauma. But no matter where a loveless person feels their lovelessness is rooted, being a loveless aromantic person is a real, true, and fully human experience. It, like all of the experiences across the aromantic and asexual spectrums, is just one of the many ways we can be in the world.

Acknowledging loveless aromantics is, of course, important because we want to be inclusive of all the ways to be ace or aro, and loveless aros are often excluded from conversations about aspec experience. But including loveless aros is also important because it opens an important set of possibilities about relationships.

It's one thing for us to say romance and sex are not necessary for the building of real and valuable relationships. This expands our possibilities in a number of ways. But to go further and say that not only are romance and sex not necessary for the building of real and valuable relationships but *love* isn't necessary either is a further expansion, and a pretty bold one. Loveless aros build relationships of all kinds, and they do it without including love. That's a radical view of relationship possibilities, and it's important to keep it in mind when we talk about what's possible for ourselves and for others.

Can a relationship include sex without romance or love?

Yes, a relationship can include sex without also including romance or love.

In the broadest sense, ace or allo, a relationship can include sexual components without also including romance or love, if the relationship partners agree on those terms. We can build relationships of all kinds—friendships, friends with benefits, casual dating relationships, and the like—that have sex as a component even if romance or love is absent or doesn't figure significantly. Do we societally treat these kinds of relationships respectfully? Not really. Society often discourages these kinds of relationships, painting them as relationships to discard on our way to more mature, complete relationships (the kinds that are exclusive romance-inclusive relationships that are moving towards marriage). Or, worse, society paints these kinds of relationships as deviant, dirty, morally corrupt, and shameful. This is sex negativity in action.

Through an aspec lens, allosexual aromantics exist. It's possible for one to feel sexual attraction in all its glory but not experience romantic attraction. For allosexual aromantics, relationships that include sex but not love and romance feel perfectly natural. So they're, of course, possible. But allosexual aromantics run into the same admonitions about the nature of romance-less relationships that include sex as everyone else does.

Why the admonitions? Remember that society has a deep obsession with relationship outcomes. Society is very invested in the fact that the relationships you inhabit produce tangible benefits for the world at large. And one of those benefits is offspring, the *next* generation of folks who'll sort into relationships that produce tangible benefits for the world at large. So yeah, society is big on us having sex, but it's big on us having sex *within the context of a long-term committed romantic relationship*, where the production of offspring is part of the set of expectations. If you take romance and love off the table, you're only having sex for fun. And society is not interested in you only having sex for fun.

That's why allosexual aromantics can face such challenges in building certain kinds of relationships. Prospective relationship partners will feel that a relationship won't be worth pursuing if the sex doesn't come with love. But the presence of romance or love doesn't make a relationship better or more meaningful than others. The presence of romance or love doesn't make sex more meaningful than sex in relationships without it. The imperative that sex and romance must exist together is a social imperative that does not reflect the true spectrum of what's possible in human relationships.

If we have sex positivity and sex negativity, do we have romance positivity and romance negativity?

Yes, romance positivity and romance negativity exist, although they are present in different degrees from sex positivity and sex negativity, and they hold some slight variations in meaning.

Romance positivity is the attitude that whatever ways consenting partners engage in romance is healthy and good. It's similar in function to sex positivity, although romance doesn't have the same level of widespread societal scrutiny as sex. Romance is generally considered to be a good thing, so romance positivity is less something folks have to learn to adopt. It is more a social attitude that challenges and marginalizes aromantic folks who aren't interested in romance.

Romance negativity is the attitude that there is something inherently wrong with romance, and that choosing to not participate in romance is a demonstration of superiority to romance-enjoyers. It's an attitude that addresses one hierarchy by creating another, which is never the true answer to eliminating hierarchies. Is romance negativity a widespread attitude? No. But when it is present, it can create a damaging stigma around some of the choices people make in their relationships.

While sex positivity and sex negativity are widespread attitudes due to the often contradictory messages everyone gets about sex, romance positivity and romance negativity are more present in aromantic communities. It's there that their impact can be more deeply felt. Romance-repulsed aromantic folks can feel pressured or shamed by romance positivity coming from alloromantic or romance-favorable aromantic folks. Romance-favorable folks can feel unnecessarily diminished or shamed by romance negativity coming from romance-averse or -repulsed folks.

What's the ideal? Holding an attitude about romance that considers all relationships to romance and love equally valid, equally worth respecting, and equally worth pursuing. Whether one wants to include romance in their relationships or whether one chooses to exclude it, those choices are equally weighted. No choice is better than another. No choice affords one superiority over another.

Things cupioromantics hear (and how to answer them)

Cupioromantics are aromantic folks that don't feel romantic attraction but do want to have romantic relationships. One might think cupioromantic is just another word for romance-favorable, but other aromantic folks can be cupioromantic. Romance-neutral folks can still want romantic relationships. And even romance-averse or romance-repulsed folks could still consider themselves cupioromantic if those feelings don't prohibit them from wanting and pursuing romantic relationships.

"So your feelings for me are fake?" Cupioromantic folks can be accused of entering into romantic relationships with "fake" feelings. If there's no romantic attraction, a relationship partner might think, then all of these romantic gestures and rituals must be simply pretend? A useful strategy here is to reassure your relationship partner that romance isn't the only form of connection that can exist between people. All of the fun things that come with romantic relationships—all the gestures, all the rituals, all the activities—can be authentically done in support of other feelings. You don't have to feel romantic feelings for someone to engage in the social dance of romance with them. If you love them, if you feel deep care for them, you can still authentically show up in romantic situations. If you want to.

"So if you're in a romantic relationship with me, I guess you're

not really aromantic anymore." It's very easy for alloromantic folks to simply focus on behaviors to define someone's romantic orientation. Aspec folks know that behavior is important but not the single deciding facet. But for allo folks, that distinction is sometimes hard to see. An alloromantic partner might see a cupioromantic partner's willingness to be romantic as a signal their aromantic identity is less true. Be clear with an allo partner that being a cupioromantic person is every bit as aromantic as being someone who's romance-repulsed. Your aromantic truth doesn't evaporate when you engage in romantic behaviors. Reinforce how important it is for any partner you have to hold space for your aromantic truth, even if you're engaging in a romantic relationship.

"Wait, you were okay with this before, and now you're not? Is there something wrong with me?" This is also rooted in the assumption that aromantic folks become "less aro" when they engage in romantic relationships. Our comfort levels with romance can change, our interests in certain romantic things can ebb, and our relationship to romance can evolve over time. Those changes, to an allo partner, can look less like the natural shape of the aro experience and more like a response to some failing in them. Communicate that fluidity is a real part of being cupioromantic, since our relationship to romance is rooted in things other than romantic attraction. Make sure you and your relationship partner discuss what fluidity has looked like for you in the past and what it looks like for you as you experience it in the present. Establish an expectation that fluidity is just a fact and not a judgment.

Things romance-repulsed aros hear (and what to say to them)

Romance-averse and romance-repulsed aros experience some of the most difficult marginalization.

"We can't have a real relationship if it's not romantic." This is amatonormativity in action. There are two important responses here. First, communicate that this belief about what makes a relationship "real" is not only inaccurate—it's just a reflection of normative thinking and not of the actual possibilities of relationships—but also diminishing and dehumanizing for aromantic people. This thinking excludes aromantics completely from the notion of "real relationships," and the relationships aro people seek out and create are as real as any other. Second, it's essential we don't internalize these kinds of responses. Aromantic folks often absorb this type of rejection as a reflection of their reality and their worth, but these rejections say *nothing* about the worth of an aro person. It speaks to the lack of understanding and knowledge in the other person on aro experience. *Don't internalize this thinking.* It doesn't reflect any truth about you and your relationship possibilities.

"So what's in a relationship if there's no romance?" This moment could be used as a teaching moment, introducing this person to the true spectrum of relationship possibilities that exist outside of love and romance. But more importantly, this is a moment to articulate what relationships look like *for you*. Talk about what you enjoy in relationships. Talk about what you're excited about providing in a relationship. Talk about what you'd hope to get in return. Be specific and personal. Share what makes relationships matter *to you*. It's one thing to talk about these possibilities in the abstract. It's another to articulate what they might mean in real terms for the real people having the conversation. This is more than just teaching. This is an expression of pride. This is a way to show that you are not ashamed of what you want and that you take joy in the things you want. It's so important for aro folks to not feel as though we must apologize for what we want. Sharing those wants confidently is a way to express that.

"I can't prioritize my relationship with you anymore. I found a romantic partner." While it's important to hold space for people to make the decisions about their relationships that work for them, it's also important to know that you deserve to have your feelings and concerns considered and respected. Often, aromantic folks are expected, and sometimes *demanded*, to understand and accept when care, connection, and companionship are pulled away from them and given to a romantic relationship. But you deserve space to share the feelings this causes. If it causes you pain, you deserve the space to share that pain. If it causes you sadness, you deserve the space to share that sadness. Approach your relationship partner and say, "While I can't tell you what decisions to make for your relationships, I think I deserve some space to tell you how this makes me feel." You can also ask, if the relationship seems to allow it, for a collaboration to address the change. "I'd like to talk about ways we might meet in the middle, because this relationship means a lot to me" is a good way to approach this subject. Just remember that you don't have to suffer in silence. Being aromantic does not mean you have to accept being pushed aside.

Reflect and Act

Reflect: What attitudes do I hold towards romance for myself? What attitudes do I hold toward romance for other people? What do I think about romance as a broader cultural idea or force? How do these attitudes work together to shape the behaviors I choose? If I could decide what attitudes and expectations society held around romance, what would I include? What would I exclude? Are there ways to take these ideas and bring them into my relationships?

Act: Get unromantic! So many of the ways we're taught to express our affection for others is through gestures and actions we consider "romantic": buying gifts, giving greeting cards, getting flowers, etc. We carry these gestures over into other relationships as well. Make a list of unromantic gestures you can do for people in your life, and do them. Offer to help with chores. Pick up a household item they're running low on. Remind them to drink more water. Find unexpected and unromantic ways to support and show care for the people in your life.

Chapter 10

Queerplatonic Relationships, Nonamory, and Relationships in the In-Between

Brent was one of my closest friends in college. We met at the auditions for a musical my college theater department was producing, and we hit it off right away. During the auditions we got paired up a lot—the show included a pair of fathers who were longtime friends—and we eventually were cast in the show together. We'd play those two fathers and basically have all of our scenes and songs together.

Needless to say, rehearsals solidified our connection pretty quickly. We had loads in common. We enjoyed each other's company. We made each other laugh a lot. And we made a solidly funny song-and-dance team in the musical. We started spending a ton of time together outside of rehearsal, too. Eventually, our mutual friends always expected to find us together. They even resorted to inviting us to house parties or group activities as a pair. If this had been the opening stretch of a queer YA romcom, the two of us would have been smooching and professing our love to each other by the final page.

But Brent was straight. I was not. Our relationship did not take on any kind of romantic or sexual components. I sometimes wished they did, but those wishes were very fleeting. I was honestly very content with the time and care I shared with Brent. Our relationship was really fulfilling to me. And I assume it was the same for him. He dated other people during the time we'd hang out, but he still always prioritized time with me. Our relationship wasn't pushed to the side when a girlfriend was in the picture. (I always really appreciated that.)

Brent graduated two years ahead of me, and when he graduated, he got a job out of state. We were both really bummed about our awesome friendship being derailed by life, but that's how it goes, right? On the day before he moved away, we had coffee as a final hangout.

As we walked to our cars, Brent stopped me.

"One sec," he said. "I want to give you something."

Brent dug a fist into his pocket and pulled out a little strip of green fabric. It was the name tag from one of his ROTC uniforms that he'd cut off to give to me.

"Here," he said. "I don't know, just...if you want it."

Of course I did. I took it. I told him thank you. And I gave him the biggest, longest hug I'd ever given anyone in my life up to that point.

Throughout my life, I've talked about my relationship with Brent as a friendship, albeit a really, really important one. But I've come to see that relationship differently these days. We were friends, yes. But we also cared for each other in ways other than friendship. We developed some very deep emotional bonds that sat somewhere beyond what we could conventionally define. It was more than a friendship. But it wasn't a romance. It was a relationship in the In-Between, defying conventional relationship structures and being something uniquely its own.

Not every relationship in your life will fall into set conventional structures of platonic, sexual, or romantic relationships. Some relationships you find yourself in will exist somewhere in that In-Between. You may also find yourself, at certain points in your life or with certain people, wanting to intentionally create relationships that don't fit into those conventional forms.

This chapter is all about those relationships that exist in the In-Between, the space where the lines between platonic, romantic, and sexual attractions get blurred.

Let's talk about alterous attraction

So if we're in a place where platonic, romantic, and sexual attractions are blurred, what kind of attraction is going on here?

It might be *alterous attraction*.

Alterous attraction is a kind of attraction a person feels when they desire an emotional closeness, but it's not platonic or romantic. Alterous attraction can feel a bit of both and neither. It's an attraction that doesn't neatly fit into any of the normative boxes we have at our disposal. Alterous attraction can also be used to refer to attractions that don't relate to any other kind of attraction. If the attraction you're feeling is undefinable, "alterous" is a good word to encompass it.

What's the value of talking about alterous attraction? Most people see attraction as being clearly delineated into discrete boxes like "platonic," "romantic," and "sexual." Even our more expansive model of attraction, including a broad spectrum of attractions, operates under the assumption that every attraction we have will fit into a defined space.

But what about human experience ever adheres neatly to boxes? Alterous attraction is an important acknowledgment that even when we work to articulate a broad spectrum of experience beyond restrictive structures like binaries, there are experiences in the human condition that remain unclassifiable. There are attractions we feel that remain in the In-Between. Alterous attraction is a way to name that.

Alterous attraction is also aspec-inclusive. It acknowledges that the spectrum of ways that ace and aro folks can experience attraction can lead to experiences of attraction in the gray area. Non-normative experiences of sexual and romantic attraction can open pathways to other non-normative experiences of attraction. Alterous attraction holds space for that.

Are all of the relationship options to follow rooted in alterous attraction? Not necessarily. Alterous attraction can be a part of them, but it's not the basis for them. Beginning with alterous attraction is not saying that everything that's not platonic, romantic, or sexual is alterous. It's just a way of stepping into a space where other feelings, connections, and relationships are possible.

What are queerplatonic relationships?

Queerplatonic relationships (also known as QPRs) are relationships that blur the boundaries between platonic, romantic, and sexual relationships. QPRs are relationships that push past the expectations of a platonic relationship but are also not contained by the expectations of romantic and sexual relationships. QPRs can contain a number of pieces of different kinds of relationships, and they can exist at multiple levels of commitment and longevity. But they blend these components in ways that reject the norms we have around what is platonic, what is romantic, and what is sexual. They're all and none. They're uniquely their own thing.

Queerplatonic relationships evolved in the asexual and aromantic communities to address the ways ace and aro folks experienced, desired, and built relationships. It's a relationship structure that directly acknowledges that ace and aro experiences are not limiting to the development of a relationship. It acknowledges that ace and aro experiences shape connection and commitment in unique ways.

Queerplatonic relationships can contain elements of romance and sex, but they do not define the nature of the relationship as the people in it define and understand it. A QPR isn't just a "fancy word for friendship." QPRs can take many forms, and a QPR can assume the same space and function as marriage does for those who choose to marry. Queerplatonic relationships are as real and authentic as any other kind of relationship.

Why would someone choose a queerplatonic relationship?

Queerplatonic relationships might represent the best relationship structure for a person to express their attractions. For aroace folks, QPRs are a relationship structure that honor how sexual and romantic attraction fits into their lives while making space for them to form the kinds of connected commitments they want. For folks who might experience sexual or romantic attraction in lesser ways but do experience other attractions in more primary ways, QPRs are a relationship structure that allows them to center those kinds of attraction. And since we don't universally feel sexual or romantic attraction for everyone, QPRs become a relationship possibility when the things we feel for someone defy our usual expectations or when what we feel is unexplainable or undefinable. In a QPR, we can build connection and commitment around all different kinds of feelings.

Queerplatonic relationships also fill a need for relationship structures that reach beyond what our norms tell us we should strive for. QPRs can be exclusive, two-person relationships where each partner is the primary for the other. QPRs can also exist in polyamorous configurations, where multiple partners form unique-to-them networks of connection all grounded in mutual feelings that aren't quite platonic, romantic, or sexual. QPRs can take the form of whatever the partners involved need and want, and they can do so without being beholden to some of the norms that surround sexual and romantic relationships. Queerplatonic relationships embrace a multitude of possibilities beyond what platonic, romantic, and sexual relationships can be on their own.

Nonamory

Nonamory is a term to describe a person's relationship style in which they do not seek out or engage in committed, long-term partnering relationships. A nonamorous person might build their lives around friends, family, and workmates, but never seek out someone or multiple someones to create relationships they center long-term.

A nonamorous person may choose to center their lives around solitary endeavors and limit the number of relationships they engage in as much as possible. For the nonamorous person, there is no central relationship that occupies a space of primacy among their relationships. There's no platonic life partner, no queerplatonic life partner, no romantic life partner.

It's important to note that nonamory is not exclusively an aspec idea. An allosexual or alloromantic person could also be nonamorous. Nonamory describes a *relationship* orientation, not a sexual or romantic orientation, so it can apply across the allo/aspec divide. But holding space for nonamory is important in this context since it's a valid way one might express their aspec identity.

Nonamory does not mean, implicitly, "no relationships of any kind ever." It would honestly be pretty challenging to exist in the world without any relationships at all. Nonamory is focusing on the absence of wanting a central relationship, a foundational partnership around which you organize your life. Nonamory is about preferring to receive one's emotional needs through a network of decentralized relationships that aren't intricately tied up in your own life.

Why would someone want to be nonamorous?

We often talk about the options aspec folks have for relationships in the context of two tracks: the track where aspec folks choose to inhabit normative relationship structures for their primary relationships and the track where aspec folks choose alternate relationship structures for their primary relationships. This display of choice is important. Many aspec folks want to find primary relationships in their lives, and laying out the options for what that looks like helps them envision relationships for themselves.

But that display of choice still centers the idea that a primary relationship, a relationship that sits at the center of our lives and grounds us in our practical and emotional wellbeing, is something everyone will want. That's just not the case. Not everyone wants to center their lives around a primary relationship. Not everyone wants their practical and emotional wellbeing focused in one relationship, and that's where nonamory presents a viable alternative vision.

It is possible to spread out practical and emotional wellbeing across a number of relationships that don't occupy a primary position in our lives. We can have a strong friendship network, a close relationship with our family, and a number of other people who address our needs and wants, all working together to fulfill our lives. This can be a large, branching network, if that's what suits us. Or it can be a very small network that allows us to live more solitary and private lives. Whatever its size, it's another way to practice relationships, and it's every bit as real as any other.

Aplatonic

Someone *aplatonic* does not experience platonic attraction and does not experience a desire to form friendships.

Why is aplatonic important to include here? Often in conversations about ace and aro relationships, there's a tendency to focus on friendship and platonic relationship as a universal fallback for aspec folks. "It's okay if you don't want sexual or romantic relationships," the argument goes, "because you can have friends! You can have platonic relationships!"

It's important to hold space for folks for whom platonic attraction and platonic relationships aren't on the table. Friendship and platonic relationships aren't a universal fallback. They're an option, certainly. But it's important to hold space for those folks who don't have those relationships as options. Being aplatonic is a valid way of being in the world, and it's a valid foundation upon which to build relationship networks.

Amatopunk

There's an aromantic term that was coined by a Tumblr user named kenochoric that I want to include here, because it encapsulates a spirit of invention and play that's important in this realm of relationships in the In-Between.

Amatopunk describes an attitude of challenging the notions of what it means to be in a relationship, what it means to experience love, and what it means to give any relationship social importance. Amatopunk rejects the idea that relationships of any kind are necessary. It rejects the idea that love must be experienced in specific ways. It believes that distinctions between different kinds of relationships are ultimately meaningless. It challenges our nuclear notions of family. It holds that all of the ways in which we connect with other people and order those connections are valid and worthy of respect.

What I like about amatopunk is its joyful embrace of the In-Between. It fully and enthusiastically embraces the idea that queer relationships can be an act of invention and that queer love and care can be acts of radical imagination.

More relationship options from the In-Between

The ace and aro communities have been prolific in their creation of language to describe the intricacies and uniquenesses of aspec experience. Asexual and aromantic microlabels provide a rich dictionary of terms aspec folks can use to describe their individual identities beyond the basic terms on the spectrums. And the aromantic community has come up with some useful language to talk about different kinds of relationships and connections.

Let's look at a few of them here.

An *aromate* is a platonic friend that fulfills the role of a soulmate in a non-romantic way. What's interesting about "aromate" is that it not only finds an aromantic option for a relationship partner, but it also locates an aromantic alternative to the notion of a "soulmate."

A *foveo* is a partner in a relationship that is not inherently romantic or platonic, but does include sexual attraction or intimacy. "Foveo" was created as an alternative to "friends with benefits," and it's an interesting creation. It conceives of that particular situation as a legitimate relationship structure of its own, instead of simply a variation on friendship. It eliminates the way "friends with benefits" suggests that friendship needs the addition of benefits, and it holds space for the idea that sexual compatibility can make a relationship without some emotional component joining it.

If you're *polyaffectionate*, you desire multiple partners that are non-romantic and non-sexual, with the consent and knowledge of all involved. Polyaffectionate is polyamory without the romance and sex, and it creates a space within a polyamory ethos for those who do not wish to have romantic or sexual connections.

And a *wavership* is a kind of relationship whose nature is fluid but its members are constant. For example, a wavership might look like two people who are in a relationship with each other, but that relationship looks like a QPR for some time, then is romantic for some time, and then is platonic for some time. Waverships can also describe relationships that experience fluidity but it's unclear what form they're taking. Waverships might exist because one or both of the relationship partners have fluid identities (like aceflux/aroflux or gray-ace/gray-aro). "Wavership" acknowledges that not only individuals experience fluidity and flux, but relationships can, as well.

There are many others like these terms. They might not catch on with broad usage, but I'm glad they're around. While these terms may never feel right for you, they represent a desire for aspec folks to name and validate the possibilities we inhabit beyond the normative structures we're pressured to fit into. These terms may feel strange or unnecessary to you at first blush, but they're assertions of ace and aro experience in the story of human experience. And they're assertions that love, connection, and care in the In-Between is as real as it is anywhere else.

Reflect and Act

Reflect: Which of the relationship structures, attraction types, or experience labels resonated with you? Did any of them feel like experiences you could claim for yourself? If so, why? Are there any relationships in your past and present that could be classified as one of the relationships discussed here? How do you think your experience of it would change if you were able to give it that name or label?

Act: Put on your educator hat. When it comes to these nontraditional, lesser-known relationship and attraction types, education means everything. Most people have never heard of most of the attractions and relationships discussed in this chapter, and people won't empathize, validate, or engage in things they don't understand. Find ways to talk about these relationship and attraction types with people you know. "You know, our friendship sometimes kind of feels like a wavership." "Have you ever heard of amatopunk? It's really neat." "I learned about this thing called alterous attraction. I'll explain it, and you tell me if you've ever felt like that before." These conversations may seem small or pointless, but they're big actions. Introducing people to the more complex world of attraction and relationships is very solid aspec advocacy.

Chapter 11

How Relationships End

Since we started this book's journey with Angelica, let me tell you how my relationship with her ended.

After gifting her the necklace that demonstrated we were in a "committed relationship," we carried on with our in-school dating life as though nothing had changed. We walked back to class together after band. We hung out at lunch sometimes. And that was pretty much that. Smooth sailing, so I was feeling pretty good about my relationship acumen.

Every fall, a traveling carnival would come through town, and I got the wild idea that Angelica and I should go to this carnival on a date. We were boyfriend and girlfriend. Carnivals were romantic. And she and I had never interacted in any way outside of our school environment. So this was a chance to take our relationship into the world and show it off. And ride the Gravitron a few times.

We were in middle school, so neither of us could transport ourselves anywhere. We relied on the kindness of parents. My parents contacted her parents, and they set up a trip for all of us to go to the carnival together, which would allow our parents to check each other out and would allow Angelica and I to go off on our own for a bit and do the whole date thing.

We met Angelica and her parents at their house, and while our parents had a quick coffee to get to know the basics, Angelica and I watched TV in their family room. I was so excited. Angelica was awesome. And she was my girlfriend. And we were going to go on this really fun date to the carnival together, and we were gonna be like all the couples I saw in movies and TV shows. I was feeling very grown-up that day.

"It's cool that you're wearing the necklace," I said to her, cutting into what had been a few minutes of silence between us. "It looks good on you, and I'm glad people will see it and know you're my girlfriend."

"I don't think I want to be your girlfriend anymore."

Whoa. My little middle school heart froze. It would have been better if she had just kicked me in the face. It would have been less surprising and would have hurt a lot less.

"What do you mean?" I said quietly.

"I think I want to be Jeremy's girlfriend now," Angelica said. Jeremy was a trumpet player in our band, and even middle school me, who had no idea yet that he was going to be as gay as blazes when he was older, knew that Jeremy was hot, and I stood no chance of changing her mind. "I like you. As a friend. I just don't want to be your girlfriend."

"Uh...okay." And that was the end of that.

We ended up having a wonderful time at the carnival. We rode the Gravitron a number of times together, and while we weren't officially dating anymore, I think Angelica and I did a great job of parting amicably.

No relationship of mine after that has reached its end so well. So thanks, Angelica.

In this chapter, we're going to talk about how relationships end. We'll talk about the way aspec folks uniquely relate to the end of relationships. We'll explore some ways to determine when a relationship is ready to end and how to do it thoughtfully, kindly, and safely. And we'll look at ways to manage the emotional challenges of having someone end a relationship with us.

Ending relationships is hard. (End them anyway)

I don't think I'm telling you anything you don't already know, but it's important to start with this acknowledgment: it's hard when a relationship ends.

It doesn't matter what side of the relationship you're on, this process sucks. If you're the one ending a relationship, it's likely you're causing pain for someone else and working through some difficult feelings of your own. If you're the one experiencing the ending, you're likely processing complicated feelings of loss, guilt, anxiety, and even shame. This is true for all kinds of relationships, not just the primary ones. Friendships, work relationships, familial relationships, chosen families, activity groups—all of these relationships, when ending, can be a source of some painful stuff.

None of what follows here is a panacea to make that difficulty vanish. It'll be hard to go through the end of a relationship with or without the advice I've got for you. What's important is that you do not let that difficulty stop you from ending relationships that don't work for you.

It can be easy to stay in relationships that don't work to avoid the unpleasantness that comes with ending them. "The unpleasantness I know is better than the unpleasantness I don't," we think. "So I might as well just stick it out. At least I know how to manage this."

We deserve to be in relationships that uplift us, support us, and nurture the whole of who we are. Full stop. Where we are able, we should always choose to move toward relationships that achieve that goal, whether that means improving the relationships we're in, ending relationships that fail us, or seeking out new ones that don't.

Is this possible in every case? No. I want to hold space for the fact that not everyone is in the position to simply leave relationships that don't serve them. Sometimes there is the threat of violence. Sometimes we rely on the resources of a relationship partner to survive. Sometimes leaving a relationship situation is possible, but in doing so we put our safety in jeopardy. When our emotional, financial, or physical wellbeing is at risk by ending a relationship, it's understandable and advisable to not take that path.

Ending relationships and being aspec

Throughout this book, we've talked about the ways our normative Big Baddies exert intense pressure on aspec folks and influence the way we see ourselves and our potential for connecting with others. One of the most pervasive ways this occurs is in how that pressure shapes the way we relate to ending relationships.

We are told in countless ways that being aspec makes us unfit for relationships. Our asexuality makes us unfit for partners who will inevitably crave sex. Our aromanticism makes us unfit for partners who will need romance in order to be happy. Our perceived insufficiencies in romance and sex make our capabilities in other relationship areas suspect. If we can't provide romance or sex, what will we be able to provide that's mature and lasting? We are seen as relationship partners that are acceptable to deprioritize. Our relationships are seen as ones to "move beyond" in order to achieve "real relationships."

We are taught to think of the end of relationships in two key ways. First, we're taught to think of a relationship's end as *our fault* because we're aspec. Second, we're taught to believe that a relationship's end is something we should *expect* because we're aspec. Both of these lessons are difficult burdens to bear, and they rob us of much of the joy and excitement we should have around the relationships in our lives.

If you carry these thoughts around with you, I want you to know that they're not the result of some unique fault of yours in managing being aspec. You have them because we're socially guided to have them. You have them because they're a punishment doled out to you for not adhering to the rules of normativity. I want you to see them as an *external* force acting on you and not an *internal* failing of who you are. You don't have to believe these messages. You don't have to internalize them. And, most importantly, you don't have to live them out in your relationships.

There is nothing about aspec identity that makes the end of relationships your fault. There's nothing about aspec identity that makes the end of relationships something you should expect as inevitable. If you decide to end relationships, you should end them because they are not healthy for you, not because you think that's what's due you for being aspec. If someone ends a relationship with you, you should process their decision as the result of *their* feelings and *their* choices, not as the result of who you are at your core.

Why should relationships end?

This is a tough question, with a mostly unsatisfying answer. Why should a relationship end? It should end because you think it's time for it to end.

Relationships cannot be perfect all the time because human beings cannot be perfect all the time. In all of your relationships, you'll encounter challenges and rough spots that will raise the question "Do I want this relationship to continue?" There's no easy way to say, "Sure, when the negative experiences fall under this list of scenarios, then it's time to end it. If they fall under this list over here, then you work it out!" Those lists don't exist. Each person has to decide for themselves whether the state of a relationship, and their experience *inside* that relationship, is such that ending the relationship is the right choice.

But we can discuss some broadly defined conditions which can cause the end of a relationship, no matter its kind.

The relationship is causing harm. This harm can take the shape of physical violence. This harm can take the shape of emotional violence. The harm can be blatant and obvious to outside observers. The harm can be more subtle and harder to detect from the outside. The harm can be purposeful and intended. The harm can be incidental and unintended. If a relationship of any kind is causing you harm, that's a valid reason for a relationship to end. And it's important to note not only that "harm" takes many forms, but that harm also is in the eye of the person experiencing it. Conditions that may not be experienced as harmful to you may be experienced as harmful to your relationship partner. And vice versa. Respectful relationships hold appropriate space for any partner in a relationship to express their experience of harm and have it be believed and addressed. (We'll talk more about harm in relationships in just a bit.)

The relationship doesn't meet your needs. We grow. We evolve. We learn new things about ourselves. We recontextualize old understandings of ourselves. We're always changing, so it makes sense that our needs as an individual and our needs from relationships will change and grow as well. Sometimes a relationship we have with a partner no longer meets our needs. Maybe that's because our needs have changed and we require different things. Or maybe our needs have remained the same, but we and our partners have become different people. If these relationships occupy a lot of your resources such as time, emotional energy, or more practical resources, but they do not meet the needs you or your partner has for the relationship, it can cause the end of the relationship.

The relationship is unable to change as you change. Sometimes the changes we undergo as individuals take us in directions that our relationships can't accommodate. Think about friends who are inseparable, until one gets accepted to a college across the country. Think about a couple dating, until one partner realizes they're polyamorous and wants to explore that part of them while their partner is resolutely monogamous. Sometimes who we are and who we are reaching to become require us to step out of relationships that can't follow us down that path. The people in the relationship can be doing everything "right," but the relationship itself isn't able to keep up. This is a valid reason for a relationship to reach its end.

The relationship has come to its natural end. We often think that relationships can (or should) only end when something goes wrong.

But that's not always the case. Sometimes relationships just reach the natural end of their life cycle, and the people in them go their separate ways. And this happens in all relationship types. It can happen in casual friendships as easily as it can happen in long-surviving marriages. These kinds of endings can contain elements of reasons we've previously discussed, but they don't have to. If you and your relationship partner come to a place where you both recognize the relationship you built is coming to a conclusion, it's okay to allow that conclusion to arrive.

How do I know it's time for a relationship to end?

Wouldn't it be great if I could just give you a sure-fire list of the irrefutable signs it's time to end a relationship? (Trust me, if I had it, I'd share it with you. And I'd have spared myself a lot of unhappiness hanging around in bad relationships.)

There's no precise method for determining when a relationship has reached its end. But we can look through our Relationship Toolbox and use our tools to identify places where a relationship might be falling short of its potential.

Autonomy. Does this relationship support the exercise of my personal autonomy? Does my relationship partner limit what I can do? Where I can go? How I use my resources? Who I can have other relationships with? Do I feel as if I have control in this relationship over who I am and what I choose to do, pursue, enjoy, and experience?

Consent. Do I feel as though I am giving consent to the things that happen in this relationship? Do I feel as though my consent is respected in this relationship? Are there times when I do not give consent, but I am pressured to change my mind? Am I afraid of saying "no" in this relationship? Have there been times my "no" has been ignored? Have there been times my "no" has been a cause for retaliation? Do I feel safe asserting my consent, particularly when it comes to my body and its borders?

Boundaries. Do I feel safe and supported in sharing my boundaries? Do I feel that my boundaries are respected by my relationship partner? Do I feel that my relationship partner actively tests my boundaries? Do they ignore my boundaries? Do they make me feel as though my boundaries are wrong or unreasonable? Are the boundaries that they set a way to control my choices or behaviors?

Communication. Do I feel like our communication is a two-way street? Does my relationship partner allow me space to communicate? Do I feel heard by my relationship partner? Does my relationship partner actively negate things I communicate without really listening to them? Does my relationship partner attempt to control important conversations? Does my relationship partner always decide when a conversation is over? Do we discuss or fight about the same things over and over again? Do I feel as though our communication is successful and safe?

Commitment. Does my relationship partner make commitments and follow through on them? Does my relationship partner acknowledge when a commitment is not honored, and do they work to readjust expectations for the future? Do I trust my partner to follow through on their commitments? Does my partner ask me to make commitments I don't feel comfortable making? Am I pressured to make commitments that limit things like my autonomy or my consent? Does my partner allow me space and grace to not fulfill commitments and make adjustments for the future?

Compromise. Do I feel like our compromise is a two-way street? Do I feel like our compromise is made in good faith? Does my relationship partner uphold the terms of compromises we make? Do I feel safe and supported in saying "no"? Does all of our compromise move in the direction of my relationship partner?

Trust. Do I trust my partner? Do I feel as though my partner trusts me? Am I scared to ask for things or express concerns because I don't trust my partner to hold safe space for me? Do I make demands of my partner in an attempt to eliminate ways I distrust them? Do they make similar demands of me?

Respect. Does my partner validate who I am as a person and the identities I hold? Does my partner allow me space and support to nurture and develop who I am as a person and the identities I hold? Do I feel safe sharing new understandings and realizations about myself with my partner? Do I validate who my partner is as a person and the identities they hold? Do I allow them space to express and live those identities?

Recognition. Do I feel seen by my partner? Do I feel as though I am safe and supported to show up as my full self when I am with my partner? Does my partner also make me feel safe and supported to show up as my full self when we are with other people? Does my partner treat the most important parts of me as *essential* parts of me? Does our relationship feel like a space where the important parts of who we are can be held as valuable *and* necessary?

Care. Does my partner's affection for me feel active, or does it feel like their affection only comes in the form of words? Does my partner use their practical resources, where reasonable, to support our relationship? Does my partner use their emotional resources, where reasonable, to support our relationship? Do I support our relationship with my practical and emotional resources, where reasonable? Is our relationship space built on active affection, on *doing* in support of each other more than *talking about* supporting each other? Are my partner's words supported by their actions? Do my actions support my words?

These are just questions to think about. And even when it's not explicitly noted above, everything we should expect from our partner is something our partner should expect from us. So we should be aware of ways we might raise red flags for our partners and their relationship tool box.

Once I've decided it's time to end a relationship, how do I end it?

Once you recognize that it's time for a relationship in your life to end, you can be hit with a wall of complicated feelings over having to actually *do the deed*. Will I hurt this person? Will they hurt me in return? Will I miss them? Will I regret my decision?

But there are ways for us to end relationships that align with all of the values we held when starting the relationship. We can end relationships kindly, directly, and compassionately so that everyone involved feels taken care of and supported.

Understand your reasons and be able to articulate them. Give yourself time to think through thoroughly the reasons you want to end the relationship. Get clarity on them and be able to share those reasons with your relationship partner. This is going to be good for both of you. You'll have the confidence to start this tough conversation and to lead it with grace. Your relationship partner will be given the respect of knowing exactly why you're feeling the way you feel. And be specific. Talk about your needs. Talk about your concerns. Talk about what you feel through the lens of your relationship tools. Ground this difficult conversation in tangible things you've taken the time to really think through. It will keep both you and the conversation focused.

Don't make it about blame. When we talked about good communication, we talked about the importance of speaking from the "I." That same approach is very useful here. If your approach to ending a relationship is filled with blame, accusations, projection, and insult, you likely won't get a kind and loving reception. While you have strong feelings about the actions and attitudes of your relationship partner, if you decide to end the relationship with them, that decision is *yours*.

It's about *you*. Talk about *your* feelings, *your* decisions, and *your* boundaries around this decision. Don't get caught up in laying blame.

Ending a relationship is a two-way street. Your relationship partner is in this relationship, too. So they're going to have some feelings about its end. It's okay for your relationship partner to have a whole range of feelings: surprise, shock, disappointment, anger, hurt, embarrassment, sadness. We should do our best to hold space for those feelings with respect and care (as long as those feelings are not being used to control or change us). We can decide how we want to *respond* to those feelings. Maybe we decide to reconsider and work with our relationship partner. Maybe we decide to stick to our plan and end the relationship. Whatever we decide, we can still allow our relationship partner to have tough human feelings and treat those tough feelings with respect.

Set clear boundaries about what things look like after the relationship ends. It's important for everyone involved to know what to expect *after* things end. Do we still get to talk? Do we stay connected online? Can we end up at the same social functions? How do we talk about this with people we both know? It's very helpful to you and your relationship partner to set some clear boundaries around life after the ending. Be thoughtful about the emotional wellbeing of everyone involved, and collaborate on boundaries that keep everyone safe. You don't have to go "no contact"—unless the relationship calls for it. Just as you and your relationship partner built a relationship that worked for you, you can build what comes after it in a way that best serves the people you are.

These bits of advice work for relationships in which all of the relationship partners involved are treating each other with care and respect. But not all relationships are like this. And it's time we talk a little about those relationships that radically veer away from the good practices we've explored in this book.

Let's talk about abusive relationships

(Content warning: mentions of forms of physical, emotional, and sexual abuse)

What is an abusive relationship? An abusive relationship is one in which one or all of the partners involved treat other partners with cruelty, disrespect, force, or violence. Abuse can take a number of forms; it can be physical, emotional, sexual, or even financial. Abuse can happen one time or it can be a pattern of behavior over time. Abuse can happen in person or online. It can be something other people see or it can be skillfully hidden from anyone outside the relationship. In whatever form it takes, abuse goes against all of the skills and values we've talked about throughout this book, and it is something no one has earned or deserves. *Ever.*

What does an abusive relationship look like? Abuse can take on many different appearances. Partners who push, shove, kick, or hit you are being abusive. Partners who regularly make threats to enact that kind of physical harm are also being abusive. Partners who force you to do things you don't want to do—like engaging in sex, consuming drugs or alcohol, going certain places, or participating in certain activities—are abusive. Partners who demand control over who you talk to, how you spend your time, what you wear, what you share on social media, or what decisions you make about your future are abusive. Partners who shame you or put you down when you're alone are abusive. Partners who shame you and put you down in front of others are abusive. Abuse is when a partner actively takes away your ability to use or ignores when you use the relationship tools in your Relationship Toolbox.

Since abuse removes our agency over the tools in our Relationship Toolbox, it's so much harder to end an abusive relationship than non-abusive ones. If abuse removes our ability to give consent, set boundaries, participate in healthy communication, exercise our autonomy, and feel respect, recognition, and care, then we don't have the agency to simply end that relationship and walk away. So even with the best of intentions and all the tips and tricks in the world, leaving an abusive relationship is exponentially harder.

This is, of course, important for everyone to be aware of in relationships, but it's especially important for aspec folks to be aware of. The experience of abuse in relationships is one of the major forms of discrimination aspec folks face. Aspec folks can find themselves being forced into sexual situations they otherwise would not participate in. Aspec folks experience "corrective rape," a form of sexual assault that is driven by a belief that this abuse will fix or "correct" a person's aspec orientation. Aspec folks can experience all forms of verbal abuse due to their aspec identity—being insulted, mocked, shamed, and dehumanized—from people they are in relationships with. Aspec folks can be threatened with loss of practical and emotional support unless they engage in sexual or romantic activities their partners believe they should have.

And when we consider the intersections that aspec folks inhabit, we realize we're only touching the surface of the abuse aspec folks can face. Black asexual men and women, who are hypersexualized by a white supremacist culture, can experience heightened threats of sexual violence. The same can be said for disabled aspec folks, whose bodies are already devalued by an ableist culture and are often treated as not fully belonging to themselves. In gay and queer male spaces, men who are aspec can find themselves enduring greater pressure to acquiesce to sexual activity. And for aspec folks who are transgender, they can experience increased threat of multiple violences in a culture that both fetishizes and reviles transgender bodies.

No one who finds themselves in an abusive relationship deserves to be there. No one chooses to be in an abusive relationship, and it is likely the person in an abusive relationship will need some help getting out of it. In the resources section of this book ("For Further Learning..."), I've provided some books and websites to learn more about abusive relationships, and I've included some hotlines and organizations that help support any person, aspec or allo, who is seeking help leaving an abusive relationship.

But what if my relationship partner ends the relationship with me?

What do we do when we're on the receiving end of someone's decision to end our relationship? Here's some advice on navigating those difficult feelings.

Feel what you feel. First, allow yourself to feel the things you feel. It's unhealthy to try to shove your feelings down and push them out of sight. You won't process them, and they'll just morph into different, more complicated feelings down the road. It's also unhealthy to spend time judging yourself for having them in the first place. If you're beating yourself up over feeling hurt or sad after a relationship ends, you're just compounding the challenging moment you're having. Just let yourself feel the things you feel. They're natural to experience, they're part of what's true for you in the moment, and they're not going away through the force of your will.

Know what you feel. It's valuable to take stock of exactly what you're feeling in the wake of someone ending their relationship with you. Is it sadness? Is it anger? Is it embarrassment? Is it regret? And further, get a handle on *why* you think those are the emotions coming up. Why is it anger instead of sadness? Why am I feeling kinda happy about it? As you process your feelings, see what you can learn about your own perceptions of the relationship.

Give yourself space and time. It can feel very appealing to immediately replace an ended relationship with one just like it. Lose a boyfriend? Get another! Lose a friend? Make a new one! End a queerplatonic relationship? Hit the streets and build a brand-new one! But this kind of rebound isn't really healthy for us. Giving yourself a little space and time is important. We have to recalibrate our understanding of who we are before we dive into sharing ourselves with someone new. So take that space and time to reacquaint yourself with you. Then you can open yourself up again to new relationships.

Ask for support. You don't have to process a relationship's end on your own. Turn to the other relationships in your life for support. This is why we build relationships, right? The people in our life can help us think through our emotions, provide us care when we need it, make us laugh, help us take care of ourselves, and remind us that we don't exist solely within the confines of any one relationship. We're part of a network of people and connections, and while it sucks when one of those connections ends, we still have our other connections, in all their wonderful variety and splendor, to help us through a tough time.

What can we learn from the end of a relationship?

So are there any positives to a relationship reaching its end? Absolutely! Here are a few questions you can ask yourself to explore your own growth and evolution after a relationship is over.

What did this relationship teach me about myself? Did this relationship help me discover something I didn't know about myself? Did this relationship help me see some part of myself in a new way? Did I surprise myself in this relationship?

What did this relationship teach me about relationships? What about this relationship would I want to replicate in future relationships? What about this relationship do I know I want to avoid in the future? What parts of this relationship did I find joy in? What parts of this relationship made me feel safe? What parts of this relationship helped me grow? What parts didn't?

What did this relationship teach me about how I handle

relationships? What did I do in this relationship that I am proud of? What did I do in this relationship that I'm not so proud of? What relationship tools did I use well? What relationship tools do I need to work on? What relationship tools did this particular relationship help me develop?

The end that's really the beginning...

The first long-term romantic relationship I had lasted just over seven years.

I was the one who ended our relationship. We were folding laundry in our bedroom, and we were talking about nothing in particular. "What belongs on our grocery list?" "Are you going to see your mom this weekend?" The kind of conversations we had all the time, had been having for seven years, conversations that had over the last several years become less background noise in a fulfilling relationship and more the only song we were singing in a relationship that had run its course. It was something I'd been feeling for a while, something I'd partially been able to articulate to myself but unable to articulate out loud. But folding this particular towel on this particular day in this particular frame of mind led me to just blurt out a simple question and a painful truth.

"Hey, are you happy? Because...because I don't think I'm happy."

That moment marked the beginning of the end of our relationship. A few months later, I moved out and got an apartment of my own. We parted as friends—we're still friends to this day, and this breakup happened over 17 years ago—and occasionally we would have dinner just to check in on each other. It was important to both of us that we stay connected, because although our relationship hadn't been able to make it in the end, we still valued each other and our presence in each other's life.

At one of these dinners about six months in, he seemed cheerier than usual. When we broke up, he was really hurt and confused and a little bit blindsided by it all. He didn't stop me from ending our relationship, but he didn't really want it to happen, either. So at many of our check-in dinners, I could feel him wanting—hoping!—that I'd say I wanted to get back together. There was always a sad, tense longing hanging over our meal. But not this time.

"I met someone," he said. "I wasn't really looking for someone, but I met this guy, and I really like him." As he told me about his new romantic interest, he showed a lightness and a hopefulness I hadn't seen in him for months.

"I'm excited for you," I said, "and I'm really happy for you."

They're still together, over 17 years later, and they continue to make each other incredibly happy. The end of our relationship made space in the world for this happiness to find its way to him. Our ending was a beginning for him.

And I haven't done so bad since then, either.

We can hold such fear about endings, and it's a fear that can keep us stuck in unhelpful patterns, stuck in unfulfilling jobs, stuck in places we hate, stuck in relationships that won't let us be our full selves, and stuck in thoughts about ourselves and our possibilities that sell us so incredibly short. But sometimes we need to lean into life's endings so that paths are cleared for new opportunities, new lessons, and new relationships. It may feel like the ending of one relationship is the end of everything. But we never know what's on the other side of an ending until we do what it takes to *get* to that other side.

In all things about ace and aro relationships—from beginnings to endings, from what they're based on to what they develop into, from whom they contain to whom they impact—what matters is the expansiveness, imagination, and courage of the people who create them. The world is not interested in the relationships we want. The world does not want us to have the relationships we want. The world actively works against us building the relationships we want. And in that resistance of the world is, for us, a kind of freedom.

To have what we want, we must imagine things beyond what is offered in the world. *That can be anything we want it to be.* We can imagine ourselves into the expansive relationship types that already bloom everywhere. Or we can push ourselves to imagine whatever kinds of relationships come next. If we can see that as a freedom instead of a hurdle, we not only open ourselves to a wider world of relationships, but we open ourselves to a wider view of *ourselves*.

And every person we touch with our bold, imaginative, courageous expansive aspec self changes the way the world thinks about aspec people. Each relationship you inhabit is an aspec relationship, and you're writing the story of our communities in every single one of those relationships. That's the power you have. That's the power of you in relationship with the world.

Use your power. Use it with care. And build a better world for all of us, one relationship at a time.

One Last Thing...

We made it! You've now got a fully stocked Relationship Toolbox, and you've got a good handle on many of the relationship options that are out there waiting for you. I hope, if you take nothing else from this book, that you reach the final page with the knowledge that you are worthy of every relationship you wish to be a part of, that you have the right to ask for any relationship you desire to build, and that even though you might not see the relationship you want reflected in the world, the fact that *you* can imagine it means it's possible.

I also want to leave you with a few wishes for what awaits you out there in the world of relationships.

I wish you a caring and fulfilling relationship with yourself. No matter where you fall on the ace or aro spectrums, I hope you wrap yourself in respect, in kindness, and in care. Because you deserve those things. We are our first relationship partner, so we should, as much as we are able, show ourselves what it's like to be in a great relationship. Nothing about your aspec identity means you deserve less than that. The aspec person you are is a gift. *Know* that.

I wish you caring and fulfilling relationships with the people in your life. No matter what forms they take, from familial relationships, to friendships, to the people you bring as close to you as your own heart, I hope they truly see you for the gift you are and treat you accordingly.

You might need to help them along here and there, but you now have the skills to do that. I hope what they bring to your life is always felt as addition, never subtraction. I hope the personal relationships you nurture expand the space you have to be your truest, most authentic self. I hope the relationships you have in your life inspire you, fulfill you, and bring you joy.

I wish you caring and fulfilling relationships with your communities. I hope you find your people! And I'm not just limiting that wish to your queer communities. Yes, I want you to find support and solidarity and encouragement and care within the ace and aro communities you inhabit. Yes, I want you to find queer folks of other stripes who make you feel that your experience is as essential to the queer spectrum as any other experience. But I also hope you find a sense of belonging in every community you inhabit. Your local community. Your religious community. Your hobby community. Your political community. Whatever collective of humans you step into, I hope that collective embraces you with kindness and care. All that we deserve in our interpersonal relationships are the things we deserve in our collective relationships. And all the skills we hone for being good partners interpersonally are the skills we can use for being good members of our communities.

And finally, I wish you a caring and fulfilling relationship with the world. We can feel very small sometimes as we face the vastness of the world. Particularly when the world is showing its uglier sides: its cruelty, its ambivalence, its violence, its rage. It's easy to think that we are the insignificant partner in our relationship with the world, that we are unable to ask for what we want, to demand to be seen, to expect to receive care. But everything we expect of the people closest to us is what we can and should expect from the world. And furthermore, we have the power to *ask* for those things of the world. The mechanics are different. We don't have intimate conversations on the couch with the world. Instead, we use our voice, our vote, our collective action, our civic participation, and, when necessary, our civil disobedience. But it's a relationship all the same. And we should always feel we are within our right and power to ask the world to be the partner we know we deserve.

At the center of all of these relationships is you. I hope you recognize the power in that. You and your aspec experience sit at the heart of a far-reaching web of human relationships that start with your heart and extend as far out into the world as you're willing to assert yourself. *And you built that web of relationships!* Not only does it speak to how much potential you have to reshape the world in more aspec-affirming ways, but it speaks to what a wonder it is to be aspec. What a wonder it is for *you* to be aspec. Look at what your singular aspec experience has the potential to create! Whenever you feel that being aspec is a limitation, think of all the ways you're making a mark on the world through the relationships you steward. Your aspec identity is a part of that stewardship, and it helps the world learn, in small and large ways, the value and meaning of our ace and aro lives.

Take care. *Give* care. And remember that being aspec is an *expansion* of possibility, not a limiting of it.

As always, I'm glad you're here.

For Further Learning...

If you'd like to learn more about asexual and aromantic lives and the relationships we can build, here are some resources to keep you learning and growing.

Where you can find me...

I'm pretty easy to find on the Internet. On TikTok, YouTube, and Instagram, you can find me @AceDadAdvice. And you can find more information about my books, my workshops, and the trainings I do at www.acedadadvice.com.

Books

If you are looking to learn more about asexuality and aromanticism, here are some nonfiction books that serve as great introductions to these two communities:

I Am Ace: Advice on Living Your Best Asexual Life by Cody
    Daigle-Orians
The Invisible Orientation: An Introduction to Asexuality by
    Julie Sondra Decker

Hopeless Aromantic: An Affirmative Guide to Aromanticism by
   Samantha Rendle
Ace Notes: Tips and Tricks on Existing in an Allo World by
   Michele Kirichanskaya
*Sounds Fake But Okay: An Asexual and Aromantic Perspective on Love,
   Relationships, Sex, and Pretty Much Anything Else* by Sarah Costello
   and Kayla Kaszyca

If you've got the basics but want to take some deeper dives into
asexuality and aromanticism, here are some nonfiction books that will
expand what you know:

*Ace: What Asexuality Reveals About Desire, Society, and the Meaning of
   Sex* by Angela Chen
*Ace and Aro Journeys: A Guide to Embracing Your Asexual or Aromantic
   Identity* by The Ace and Aro Advocacy Project
Ace Voices: What It Means to Be Asexual, Aromantic, Demi or Grey-Ace
   by Eris Young
Ending the Pursuit: Asexuality, Aromanticism and Agender Identity by
   Michael Paramo
*Refusing Compulsory Sexuality: A Black Asexual Lens on Our
   Sex-Obsessed Culture* by Sherronda J. Brown
Asexual Erotics: Intimate Readings of Compulsory Sexuality by
   Ela Przybylo

If you are looking to learn more about good relationships, here are two
nonfiction books that might be helpful:

Queer: The Ultimate LGBTQ Guide for Teens by Kathy Belge and Marke
   Bieschke
*It Doesn't Have to Be Awkward: Dealing with Relationships, Consent,
   and Other Hard-to-Talk-About Stuff* by Dr. Drew Pinsky and Paulina
   Pinsky

Online learning and community

While it would be impossible to provide you with an exhaustive list of the content creators and educators' online teaching about asexuality, aromanticism, and the joys of being a part of the queer community, I want to provide you with a sampling of folks that will get you started. Again, this is just the tip of the iceberg! There are plenty of incredible creators I love and adore that aren't here. Use these accounts as springboards to find all of the amazing people out there making content about our queer community.

TikTok: @angstyace, @fluentlyaspec, @madzoffmain, @abitheace, @ace.scicomm, @asexualmemes

Instagram: @_aceingrace_, @theyasminbenoit, @acesexeducation, @zoestoller, @authorsarahwhalen, @teachingoutsidethebinary, @hicharlieocean

YouTube: Lynn Saga, The Asexual Goddess, Milady Confetti, Spacey Aces

If you want to learn more about asexuality and aromanticism, you can also find great information at these three websites:

The Asexual Visibility and Education Network (AVEN)
www.asexuality.org

Aromantic-spectrum Union for Recognition, Education, and Advocacy (AUREA)
www.aromanticism.org

The Ace and Aro Advocacy Project (TAAAP)
www.taaap.org

If you or someone you know is in need of help...

Love is Respect, a 24/7 resource powered by the National Teen Dating Abuse Hotline, offers information support and advocacy to young people experiencing abuse in their relationships. If you have questions or concerns about your relationships, and need help, Love is Respect is there for you.

Visit www.loveisrespect.org, call 1-866-331-9474, or text LOVEIS to 22522.

The Trevor Project is the country's leading suicide prevention and crisis intervention nonprofit for LGBTQIA+ young people. If a relationship in your life has reached a crisis point or you are in need of support for thoughts of suicide, The Trevor Project can provide support and connect you with help.

Visit www.thetrevorproject.org, call 1-866-488-7386, or text 678-678.